Best Wishes in your
work with the Deaf –
Henry L. Buzzard

Aug. 27, 1959.

THE EPISCOPAL CHURCH CENTER

815 SECOND AVENUE/NEW YORK, NEW YORK 10017
Telephone: (212) 867-8400   Cable Address: FENALONG, N.Y.

AN INTRODUCTION

It might be said that Thomas Gallaudet and Henry Winter Syle could be described as the "silent missionaries" of the Church. These two priests dedicated their lives and ministries to the proclamation of the Good News of God in Christ to the deaf

Their ministry to the deaf reached isolated persons and brought them into relationship with Christ and each other. Those who were "far off" due to deafness were brought near to Christ by their efforts.

I commend the efforts of Father Berg to bring forward the stories of Thomas Gallaudet and Henry Winter Syle to us all.

Edmond L. Browning
Presiding Bishop

Thomas Gallaudet

Apostle to the Deaf

by

**Otto Benjamin Berg &
Henry L. Buzzard**

*with a Supplement on
the life and ministry
of Henry W. Syle*

**Published by
St. Ann's Church for the Deaf
209 East Sixteenth St., New York, N.Y. 10003**

Printing by Maryland Lithograph, Laurel, Maryland

DEDICATION. This book is dedicated to the family of Thomas Gallaudet, particularly his deaf granddaughters Margaret Sherman Gillen and Eleanor Sherman Font; also all those who hold dear the memory of Henry Winter Syle.

Copyright © 1989 by Otto B. Berg
All rights reserved
Library of Congress Catalog Card Number: 89-85591
Manufactured in United States of America
Desk-top publishing performed by Stephen A. Brenner
Proofreading by Arthur R. Steidemann
Cover design by William Kirk Crume

Rev. Dr. Thomas Gallaudet,

Contents

Introduction

T he name Gallaudet is recognized with the highest degree of respect by deaf people throughout this country. There are three Gallaudets who have earned this respect by their significant and lasting contributions to the well-being and advancement of the deaf everywhere, yes, not only in this country but in the world. These three are:

The Rev. Thomas Hopkins Gallaudet (1787-1851), the father, who in the year 1817 founded the first permanent school for the deaf at Hartford, Ct., with the assistance of Laurent Clerc, a French-born deaf teacher.

The Rev. Thomas Gallaudet, eldest son—with no middle name or initial—(1822-1902) was a priest of the Episcopal Church whose missionary work extended all across the United States and in some measure to European countries as well.

Edward Miner Gallaudet (1837-1917), youngest child of Thomas Hopkins Gallaudet, taught in his father's school at Hartford until 1857, when he was named principal of the Columbia Institution for the Deaf and Dumb at Washington, D.C. The senior department, which was added in 1864, was named Gallaudet College, now known as Gallaudet University.

Thomas Hopkins Gallaudet and his son Edward Miner Gallaudet are better known than the Rev. Thomas Gallaudet, at least in the deaf community, but the nation-wide ministry of the latter was notable, for it contributed much to the well-being and advancement of the deaf in all areas of their lives—the spiritual, the intellectual and the social. Since there exists much biographical material pertaining to Thomas Hopkins Gallaudet and his son Edward Miner Gallaudet* this work will be concerned mainly with the life and ministry of Thomas Gallaudet, abbreviated in the text hereafter to T.Gallaudet.

My book, "A Missionary Chronicle," published in 1984, has considerable material pertaining to the ministry of T.Gallaudet, but from the deaf community have come requests for a biography of this great man, who has been referred to as the Apostle to the Deaf** in our country. It so happens that a great deal of research into the life and ministry of T.Gallaudet has been done by Mr. Henry L. Buzzard, who at one time was a librarian at Gallaudet University and then at the New York School for the Deaf at White Plains, N.Y. Mr. Buzzard put a considerable collection of his papers and notes, acquired over a period of several years and pertaining to the Gallaudets, at my disposal. These will make additional research almost unnecessary. Mr. Buzzard has stated that he was encouraged and inspired in this enterprise by two grandchildren of T.Gallaudet, Mrs. Margaret Sherman Gillen and Mrs. Eleanor Sherman Font, now deceased. Also, provided me by the Rev. Robert H. Grindrod, a former officer and executive secretary of the Episcopal Conference of the Deaf, is a print-out of "A Sketch of My Life," which was written in longhand by T.Gallaudet, probably after he retired in 1892. (The original manuscript of 53 pages is in the Gallaudet University Archives.)

Ordinarily a person's achievements are summed up in the final chapter of his or her life story. But most readers

* Thomas Hopkins Gallaudet's and Edward Miner Gallaudet's papers are in the Library of Congress (microfilm copies); also in the Gallaudet University Archives. A comparatively recent biography of Edward Miner Gallaudet is "Voice of the Deaf" by Maxine Tull Boatner, published by Public Affairs Press, Washington, D.C.
** While this was being written I was informed that at the General Convention of the Church held July 1-11 in Detroit a resolution that was brought before the convention and approved stated, in part: "Resolved, that the Calendar of the Church Year be amended to include: August 27th, Thomas Gallaudet and Henry Winter Syle, priests, 1902, 1890." (The dates refer to the year of their death, respectively.)

of a biography want to know at the onset what sets this
person apart—why does the life story come to be written?
In answer to this a few highlights of his ministry are here
given.

The Rev. Thomas Gallaudet was the founder—in 1852—of
St. Ann's Episcopal Church for the Deaf in New York City,
the first of its kind in this country. But soon afterwards
the missionary-minded priest ventured beyond New York
to establish mission congregations of deaf people in the
larger cities throughout this country, even as far west as
California.

T.Gallaudet believed that if sufficiently educated, deaf
men could qualify for holy orders in the Church and
minister to congregations of deaf people.   He was the
sponsor of Henry W. Syle, the first deaf man to receive
holy orders in the Christian Church. (In the Supplement
of this book is a biographical sketch of the Rev. Mr. Syle.)

It was not only the spiritual needs of the deaf that
concerned T.Gallaudet. He was concerned also with their
educational and social needs.   He was instrumental in
establishing three schools for the deaf in New York State,
and he gave important support to deaf founders of schools
in Massachusetts, Pennsylvania, and New Mexico.
Because he was known to have "expertise" in matters
pertaining to the education of the deaf—he was a teacher of
the deaf for 15 years, and a Board member for 36 years, in
the New York School—he was often consulted when the
need for a new school arose in other parts of the country.
He was a member of the Convention of American
Instructors of the Deaf and the Conference of Principals &
Superintendents of American Schools for the Deaf.   He
attended conventions of these two organizations; also
conventions of the Empire State Association of the Deaf
and the New England Gallaudet Association of the Deaf.
Another noteworthy accomplishment of T.Gallaudet was
the founding of the Gallaudet Home for Aged and Infirm
Deaf in the year 1872.

Since it is at the time of death that one's life
achievements and standing in the eyes of his or her

fellowmen generally comes into a focus, some facts relating to the death of T.Gallaudet are set down here.

T.Gallaudet died on August 27, 1902, just a little more than exactly two months after he had celebrated his 80th birthday—June 3—and almost exactly two months after the 50th anniversary of his ordination to the priesthood—June 28.

In a national paper of the deaf, *The Deaf-Mutes' Journal*, the editor led off an editorial in an extra edition of the paper by saying: "A friend of humankind has passed away. The best-loved and trusted friend of the deaf of this and past generations has gone to his reward. Rev. Dr. Thomas Gallaudet is at rest in Paradise and thousands of deaf-mutes are plunged in deepest sorrow."

At the funeral service over the remains of T.Gallaudet held Friday, August 29, at St. Matthew's Church near Central Park in New York City there was hardly standing room in the church according to the story in the Journal. The writer went on to say: "The vestibule at the time set for the service to begin was blocked, and in the street many more were endeavoring to get into the church. The floral tributes from friends, deaf and hearing, were magnificent, numbering upwards of two hundred pieces.... Clergy attending numbered over 50 and of these, three were deaf missionaries (even the Bishop of New York interrupted his vacation in order to officiate at this service for his dear friend).... When the services were over the casket was placed in the vestibule of the church, where it was viewed by no less than 1,500 persons, the majority of whom were deaf, and who wept as they looked for the last time on the benignant features of their beloved friend. Dr. Gallaudet was laid out in full vestments, and the entire top of the casket was removed. In a semi-circle around the head was banked a profusion of lilies of the valley, and Dr. Gallaudet looked so peaceful in his eternal sleep."

There were many testimonials to the greatness and goodness of this man. One of the most heart-warming was a letter sent to the editor of the Journal by a deaf man in Belfast, Ireland, just a few weeks after the death of T.Gallaudet. The letter is reprinted here and brings to a conclusion this introduction to the life and ministry of the Rev. Dr. Thomas Gallaudet.

Sir:—Will you kindly allow me space for a few words in reference to the impression produced on the deaf of Europe by the death of the Rev. Thomas Gallaudet, D. D.

The American people do not need to be reminded of the life-long mission work which was so earnestly and successfully carried on by the late Dr. Gallaudet—that work speaks for itself. But not many in the United States may be aware that the impetus given by this noble man to mission work among the deaf of his own land was felt in, and has left its impression on, every country in Europe, and, indeed, in the world.

Here in the British Isles many of our missions owe their existence to his example and encouragement. It was my privilege to meet our late friend on most of his European tours. I can, therefore, speak from experience. When in Europe Dr. Gallaudet never took the rest he so badly needed, but voluntarily spent his time in giving addresses and speaking at congresses, or pleading from pulpits on behalf of those who lay so near his heart—his well-beloved deaf and dumb. It mattered not to him to what nation they belonged, his heart was so large it had room for them all!

As a deaf man I am in a position to fully appreciate the blank which has been left by the passing of our saintly friend. To us he was a living link with the days when our class was considered incapable of education, or of receiving the blessed truths of religion, and his very name was a refutation of these old-world assertions, for, was not the father of our venerated "Doctor" the first teacher of the deaf in America, and was not he, himself, their first missionary?

His is now the reward of those who are "faithful unto death." All through his long life he unselfishly worked for the "children of silence," and now on the "other shore" he is greeted by an army whose ears have been loosened since he last met them here on earth. Our beloved friend has indeed entered into the "joy of the Lord."

I am, Sir, Faithfully yours, FRANCIS MAGINN, B.D., 11 Fisherwick Place, Belfast.

(Rev'd) Otto B. Berg

THOMAS GALLAUDET —

APOSTLE TO THE DEAF

CHAPTER 1

Roots

By a strange circumstance the country that in the year 1611 caused a member of the Gallaudet family to emigrate to America, a little more than 200 years later welcomed to its principal city a descendant of this emigrant and provided for him at a Paris school the basics for the instruction/education of the deaf. The director of the school, Abbé Roch-Ambrose-Curran Sicard, even went so far as to permit one of his star teachers, a deaf man named Laurent Clerc, to accompany this member of the Gallaudet family—Thomas Hopkins Gallaudet—on his return trip to America so that the two could establish at Hartford, Ct., in the year 1817, the first permanent school for the deaf in this country. Also, in view of the political situation that existed in France during the early part of the seventeenth century that caused the exodus of thousands of Huguenots to other countries it is interesting to note that T. H. Gallaudet, a Protestant minister, while a guest of Abbé Sicard in the year 1816, was even invited to give a series of discourses[*] on various points of Christian faith and practice in the Chapel of the Oratoire in Paris.

---

[*] A copy of these Discourses is in the repository of rare books at the Gallaudet University Archives.

The emigrant who left France in 1611 was named Pierre Elizee Gallaudet, born of Joshua and Margaret (Prioleau) Gallaudet, who with their family lived at Mauze, just 20 miles east of La Rochelle at the time of the revocation of the Edict of Nantes.* Pierre Elizee Gallaudet, a doctor, came to New York and was one of the founders of New Rochelle in the early 1700s.

The genealogy of the Gallaudet family that follows is from "Voice of the Deaf" by Maxine Tull Boatner, published in 1959 by Public Affairs Press, Washington, D.C.

> Pierre Elisee and his wife Jan had several children—among them a son Thomas, born in 1724, who married Catharine Edgar of Rahway, N.J., in 1753.... Thomas and Catharine Gallaudet had six children, all born in New York. Their second child, born April 21, 1756, was named Peter Wallace Gallaudet. At an early age he settled in Philadelphia.

> Peter Wallace Gallaudet went into the mercantile business. His earliest activities in Philadelphia are not recorded except for one fact found in a grandson's diary: he once acted as private secretary to George Washington. Early in 1787 he was married to Jane Hopkins in her Hartford, Ct., home....

> Twelve children were born to Jane and Peter Gallaudet. The first eight were born in Philadelphia and the others in Hartford following the family's move to Connecticut in 1800. The first child was Thomas Hopkins Gallaudet, born December 10,1787. Thomas was 13 years old when his parents settled in Hartford, where they lived in Prospect Street among a group of families of varied characteristics but united by ties of common heritage. Here lived the wealthy

---

* The Huguenots probably received their name from a Swiss religious leader named Bezanson Hugues. Because France was Catholic the Huguenots, who believed the teaching of John Calvin, were persecuted and many even murdered. When Henry III, a Catholic king, was assassinated Henry Of Navarre, a Huguenot, became king, but the new king decided to become a Catholic so he could rule better. However he was still sympathetic to the Huguenots and in 1598 issued the Edict of Nantes. This law gave the Huguenots freedom of worship in about 75 towns and cities. They were also given complete political freedom. The Huguenots then formed a sort of Protestant republic within the Catholic kingdom. Unfortunately, in 1685 Louis XIV repealed the Edict of Nantes. Thousands of Huguenots fled France to new homes in England, Germany, Holland and America.

and cultured Daniel Wadsworth, and Dr. Mason Fitch Cogswell, who was to play such an important part in the life of young Thomas, was a neighbor....

Peter Gallaudet* and his family made their home in Hartford for 15 years before moving to New York City, where his wife Jane died. After a brief stay in Philadelphia during the early 1820s he moved for the last time in 1824 to Washington D.C., where he lived for almost a score of years, occupying a position in the Register's office in the United States Treasury until his death in 1843....

Mrs. Boatner relates that Thomas Hopkins Gallaudet, after attending Hartford Grammar School, entered Yale College, from which he graduated with a A.B. degree. After trying to "find his niche" in the world and traveling about—as far south as Kentucky—he returned to Hartford in 1811. Thereupon he decided to enter the newly opened Andover Theological Seminary to prepare himself for the ministry. In 1814 he graduated from the seminary after giving himself to intense study....

It was about this time that he became interested in the daughter of his Hartford neighbor, Dr. Mason Cogswell. Alice Cogswell was a child of nine who had lost her hearing earlier as a result of a fever. His first visit with her was in his family's garden, where she was playing with her younger brothers and sisters. It intrigued the young minister to communicate with her, particularly since she showed a marked aptitude for learning. Her father had in his library a book written by the Abbé Sicard of the Royal Institution for Deaf Mutes, and he let T.H.G. practice its contents with Alice. Thomas showed ingenious aptitude in communicating with the child, and he taught her many simple words and sentences. A local poet, Lydia Huntley Sigourney, also had been able to gain Alice's confidence and had given her lessons. The success of these attempts made her father more painfully aware that not only his daughter but other deaf children should have some means of obtaining an education.

---

* The remains of Peter Wallace Gallaudet, who died in 1843, are buried in the Congressional Cemetery, Washington, D.C., near the tomb of John Philip Sousa, at one time director of the U.S. Marine Band.

An investigation of the situation of deaf people in Connecticut, headed by Dr. Cogswell in 1812, revealed that there were 84 deaf and dumb—as the deaf were then called—in Connecticut alone, and then he and his friends came to the conclusion that in the United States there were at least several thousand such persons; "and in all the country there was not means of educating these deaf people."

As a result, in 1815, the Rev. Thomas Hopkins Gallaudet was invited by a group of prominent Hartford citizens to visit Europe to learn the art of teaching the deaf. After some misgivings he decided to make preparations for the journey and on May 25, 1815, he sailed on the tiny vessel named *Mexico* to seek in other countries ways and means of educating the deaf. It is interesting to note that he had taken along the book by the Abbé Sicard on methods of educating the deaf.

After a month-long journey Thomas Hopkins Gallaudet landed in Liverpool, the beginning of the European tour that would take him to London, Oxford, Birmingham, Edinburgh and finally Paris. Mrs Boatner then relates:

> In England and Scotland he was bitterly disappointed to find that the teaching of the deaf was a monopoly confined to the Braidwood family; and there was neither the money nor the time to serve the years of apprenticeship required. Fortunately, while in London, he met the Abbé Sicard, who invited him to Paris as a guest of his institution. Thomas had already seen enough of "method" in English classrooms to realize that the English concentrated on teaching the deaf to speak; from Sicard's textbook he knew that the French teachers relied upon the Abbé de l'Epée's creation of a system of signs in which a "sign" stood for a word.

Thomas Hopkins Gallaudet remained in England until the spring of 1816, partly because of the disturbing political situation in France caused by Napoleonic wars. On March 5th he sailed from London and on March 9th he arrived in Paris where Sicard received him with open arms. "All facilities of the Paris institution were put at his disposal. The Abbé arranged to give him lectures three times a week; he attended classes at all times, observing and learning the sign language from the expert Paulmier...."

When T.H.Gallaudet prepared for his homeward journey, the Abbé Sicard yielded to the entreaties of Laurent Clerc, who asked to be released from his position in the Paris institution to return and help Gallaudet found the first (permanent)* school for the deaf in America. Clerc was to be the first educated deaf man to walk the streets of this country, and his presence encouraged the establishment of the French method of signs and finger spelling that became the basis for the democratic Combined System of teaching this specialized work subsequently practiced by the residential schools for the deaf in the United States. T.H. Gallaudet combined the voice, the eye, and the hand, to found America's own system.

These two pioneering spirits sailed from Le Havre June 18, 1816, on the Mary Augusta. Clerc learned to write English during the month's journey, and was capable of answering any question put to him upon his arrival in the States. He and Gallaudet spent the next seven months speaking, raising funds, and getting the American Asylum for the Deaf and Dumb ready to receive its first pupils. The doors were opened April 15, 1817, and at once attracted outstanding visitors. James Monroe, then President of the United States, paid his respects to the institution when he visited Hartford in 1817. Henry Clay, Andrew Jackson and Charles Dickens made the American Asylum part of their itinerary; when Mrs. Anne Royall wrote her travel book after touring the States, she referred to the school as "the Glory of Hartford, and indeed that of America."

Much more could be set down here about the life of T.H.Gallaudet, who gained national prominence after the establishment of the school at Hartford, but for the purpose of this work it need only be added that it was at

* The Hartford school was preceded by the abortive attempt of John Braidwood, grandson of the famous educator, Thomas Braidwood, of Scotland, to conduct a school at Cobbs Manor in Chesterfield County, Virginia. An outgrowth of the private class taught as early as 1812 by Braidwood in the home of Colonel William Bolling at Bolling Hall, an estate some miles farther up the James River in Goochland County. The Cobbs school was opened to the public on March 1, 1815. It closed in the autumn of 1816.--From "History of the Education of the Deaf in Virginia" by R. Aumon Bass, c1949, Virginia School for the Deaf and the Blind, Staunton, Va.

the school that romance entered his life and thus he became also a family man. Mrs. Boatner tells it in this way:

> There is no record of romance in Thomas' life until after he became principal of the American Asylum. The tender passion was in the offing, however, from the moment he went to New Haven to interview a father who had two deaf daughters he wished to enter in the school. Miner Fowler and his family lived at Guilford, Ct. Their daughters, Sophia and Parnell, were among the first students to be entered on the school roster. Sophia was 19 and had never received any formal schooling. When the 31-year-old principal was introduced to this amazing child-woman he marveled at once at the grasp of her mind.
>
> Before Sophia Fowler had been three years in the school T.H.Gallaudet had given her his heart completely. He consulted her parents and asked that she be allowed to live in the city so that he might conduct a true courtship. Sophia, now 23, was happy in her mentor's promise to continue her instruction after their marriage, which took place on August 29, 1821....

To this union were born eight children. The eldest was Thomas; the youngest was Edward Miner.

So we come now to the subject of this book—the Reverend Thomas Gallaudet, whose roots, beginning in 1611 with a family of French Huguenots, have been here been set down.

CHAPTER 2

Foundation Stones

I n "A Sketch of My Life" the Rev. Thomas Gallaudet
stated that he was born in Hartford, Ct., June 3, 1822.
He writes about the school for the deaf that was founded
by his father, Thomas Hopkins Gallaudet (T.H.G. for
short), who was also principal for 14 years. In the Sketch
he further stated: "My mother, Sophia Fowler, of Guilford,
Ct., was a member of the first class received into this
institution. She responded so gracefully and effectually to
my father's instruction that she won his heart and became
his wife.... My mother being deaf mute, I do not remember
when I began to use the sign language."

It can be seen from this then that at an early age
T.Gallaudet could communicate fluently in both sign
language and in spoken English. In fact this must have
been true of all the children, for he said, "We conversed
with our deaf–mute mother by manual methods as well as
we did with our father by speech." But being the eldest

child of the family it was T.Gallaudet who, in the absence of his father, acted as the interpreter for his deaf mother when visitors without a knowledge of sign language came to the Gallaudet home; also, when the mother went shopping for food or clothing she would take T.Gallaudet along to facilitate communication with salespersons.

Perhaps this arrangement permitted the father to spend more time each day in his office and attending to the many responsibilities in the management of the school. The father, as the teacher-administrator, had to decide whom he should hire as teachers—college graduates, yes, but they must accept new ideas and learn sign language; which deaf children should be admitted; where to get funds for the support of the school. In selecting students, T.H.G. wanted those with a sound mind and be above-average in intelligence. Their excellent achievements meant, of course, the success of the school and attracted funds for its support from all sources. In this respect the presence of the deaf Frenchman Laurent Clerc provided T.H.G. not only with an outstanding teacher but a role-model of a deaf man who had achieved success in the world.

The Gallaudet home was noted for its hospitality, and of this Edward Miner Gallaudet, brother of T.Gallaudet, wrote in his "Life of Thomas Hopkins Gallaudet,"[*] their father:

> My father believed that one of the most important elements in the education of a family was the making of the home a resort for interesting and entertaining people. And though he could never indulge in expensive hospitality the number of guests who slept under his roof and ate at his table was legion. It was always spoken of with surprise among the children when the spare room was empty.
>
> His children were taught to show equal courtesy to the black missionary from Africa and the white diplomats from Europe. Dr. Yang Wing, well–known as a distinguished graduate of Yale College, a mandarin of high rank in China, the promoter of the American education of Chinese youth

---

[*] "Life of Thomas Hopkins Gallaudet, Founder of Deaf-Mute Instruction in America" by Edward Miner Gallaudet. Published by Henry Holt and Co. 1888.

and diplomat, described one of the most unforgettable experiences as a guest of the Gallaudet family.

"The entire domestic family surroundings carried with them a heavenly atmosphere, and no one was present in that home on Prospect Street, either immediately after breakfast or after tea in the evening, when all the members met together, could have failed to be charmed with the scene."

"Then came Mrs. Gallaudet. I remember she was the last member of the family to whom I was introduced. I was not aware at first that she was a mute; her face was full of healthful color, with large clear brown eyes that spoke volumes, though she could not give her thoughts articulate expression. She had a dignified and queen–like air, softened with a sweet smile which seemed to be perennial."

A frequent visitor at the Gallaudet home in Hartford was Alice Cogswell, whose father, Dr. Mason Fitch Cogswell, one of the most prominent physicians and surgeons in the United States during his time, influenced T.H.G. to go to schools in Europe to study their methods of teaching the deaf, then returning to America to establish at Hartford the school that became known as the American School for the Deaf. Alice was, of course, one of the first pupils enrolled and her classmate was Sophia Fowler, who became the wife of T.H.G. and so the mother of T.Gallaudet. When T.Gallaudet was 8 years old, the family received the shocking news of the death of Alice on December 30, 1830. This was just 13 days after Alice's father had died of pneumonia at the age of 69. Her death was brought on by the deep attachment that she had for her father, for she became violently ill and delirious and was unable to attend his funeral. One can easily speculate that had it not been for the little deaf girl Alice and her father the school for the deaf at Hartford would not have come into being and the education of the deaf in this country would have taken a much different turn than we know.*

In addition to his responsibilities as principal/administrator of the school for the deaf, T.H.G.

---

* *The Deaf-Mutes' Journal*, April 26, 1883. Also the *Gallaudet Encyclopedia of Deaf Persons and Deafness*, published by McGraw-Hill Book Company, 1986.

was a successful writer of religious books for children and youths. The work required that he do considerable reading of materials pertaining to religious subjects, particularly pertaining to the young, so his home was full of publications of this sort. Thus, while T.Gallaudet was still a boy he was exposed to the atmosphere and materials in his father's library. He had the privilege of reading them and discussing the subjects with his father. Religion was an important matter both in the home and at the school.

The father of T.Gallaudet was an ordained minister of the Congregational faith and although he did not have pastoral oversight of a church congregation the school became, in effect, a church, for the students were required to attend daily chapel exercises, they learned common Old Testament stories and were expected to be familiar with the parables, miracles and principal events in the life of Christ as set down in the New Testament. This is not surprising in view of the fact that when he left France in 1816 accompanied by the deaf French teacher Laurent Clerc they entered into a written contract that the curriculum of the new school should be as follows:

> Mr. Clerc shall attempt to give his pupils a knowledge of grammar, language, arithmetic, the globe, geography, history; of the Old Testament as contained in the Bible, and Jesus Christ, the Acts of the Apostles, the Epistles of St. Paul, St. John, St. Peter and St. Jude. He is not to be called upon to teach anything contrary to the Roman Catholic religion which he professes,* and in which faith he desires to live and die. Mr. Gallaudet, as head of the Institution, will take charge of all matters pertaining to religious teaching which may not be in accordance with his faith—*American Annals of the Deaf*, Vol. 24, No. 2, pg. 115.

When T.Gallaudet was 9 years old, his father resigned from the school when the Board declined to reduce his burdens;   the Board felt that there was no one else qualified to share the burdens in the new experiment—the Hartford school for the deaf. So the family moved off the

---

* Mr. Clerc, after residence of several years in this country, became an Episcopalian.-Ed. (From *Annals of the Deaf*.)

school campus to a residence in the city. It is said that the father became more attached to his children and he hired a tutor to teach the children at home as a public school system had not yet been established. After securing a fundamental education at home T.Gallaudet entered the Hartford grammar school.

In 1838 T.Gallaudet's father took a new position as a chaplain at the Retreat for the Insane in Hartford, thus giving him another source of funds for the support of the larger family. This position required him to officiate at religious services and have daily prayers for the patients, and hold conferences with them as needed. This position required only a few hours of his time each day so that he could continue his writing of religious books.

It is interesting to note that when T.Gallaudet was ordained to the priesthood and began his ministry in New York he became involved in several organizations that had been set up to provide charitable services in the city. For several years he was a member of the executive committee of the Episcopal Church City Mission Society, which was programmed to help destitute people with shelter, food and employment. Another organization was the Home for Old Men and Aged Couples, founded in 1872 and was incorporated by the Legislature of New York that year. T.Gallaudet was one of the trustees. In a sermon preached by T.Gallaudet at the celebration of the 25th anniversary of St. Ann's Church for the Deaf he said: "It was a pleasant thing for us to remember on this our twenty-fifth anniversary that in this church was held the meetings which led to the formation of the House of the Incurables, the House of Rest for Consumptives and the Home for Old Men and Aged Couples. Another noteworthy organization that T.Gallaudet founded and of which he was the chaplain and advisor was the Sisterhood of the Good Shepherd, five in number. In 1863 the sisters entered upon the work of caring for some 75 inmates of the newly-built House of Mercy, located at the foot of West 86th Street in New York. More will be said of the sisters in another chapter.

When it came time for T.Gallaudet to graduate from Grammar School he was looking forward to entering Yale

College, New Haven, the most flourishing university in the state, about 45 miles from Hartford. But of this plan he wrote in his Sketch: "I received one of the greatest disappointments of my life in my father's decision to send me to Washington College, now Trinity, and to keep me under home influence. I became a member of the freshman class of 1838 under President Gotter. How little I realized that the whole course of my life was to be changed (by this decision of my father)." Economic conditions in the home no doubt influenced his father's decision; Washington College was a local school in Hartford.

Since Trinity College was under the direction of the Episcopal Church, particularly the Diocese of Connecticut, T.Gallaudet came into contact with liturgical worship according to the Book of Common Prayer, its teaching with respect of the historic episcopate (traced back to the apostles) and other tenets of its faith. He was much impressed by the sermons of the Rev. George Burgess, then rector of Christ Church, Hartford. It appears that he became a candidate for confirmation without consulting his father and family, who were Congregationalists. This naturally was cause for disappointment and sorrow among members and friends of the family but not estrangement. Later T.Gallaudet discovered an old Book of Common Prayer that had on it the worn inscription THOMAS GALLAUDET, which was the name of his paternal great grandfather, who therefore must have been an Episcopalian. And so he could assert that he was returning to the original faith of the Gallaudets and that these Congregationalists had gone astray!

Just how serious he felt about his new-found faith may be inferred from this statement he made in his Sketch— "I was graduated in 1842 with the determination to go to the General Theological Seminary in New York with several of my classmates, but my father prevailed on me to give the whole subject a careful consideration, saying I was only 20 years old and could wait." The outcome of this was that T.Gallaudet did not go to the New York seminary to pursue theological studies, but instead took a position as a teacher in the public schools of Glastonbury and Meriden, and at the same time studying the books his father directed him to look into before he decided to leave his Congregational connection. The outcome of this is given in his Sketch— "At the end of the year it came to pass that my Church ideas were more firmly settled than ever and my father saw that it was useless to prolong the kindly controversy.   In bringing it to a conclusion, however, he persuaded me to accept a position of professor in the New York Institution for Deaf-Mutes under Dr. Harvey P. Peet."

CHAPTER 3

Fanwood

In September 1843, Thomas Gallaudet, aged 21, began his professional career as a teacher at the New York School for the Deaf, then known as the New York Institution of the Deaf and Dumb and later commonly called Fanwood.

It is worthy of note that the New York School for the Deaf, then located on 50th Street between Fourth and Fifth Avenues, was incorporated by an act of the State Legislature on April 15, 1817—the very day that the school in Hartford opened for reception of pupils. The *Deaf-Mutes Journal* of April 12, 1917, said in an editorial respecting this: "The vitally important event of the establishment of the School for the Deaf in New York, crowned with deserved honor and success the efforts of one of the really great philanthropists of his day and generation, the Rev. John Stanford, D.D. This remarkable man was the originator of at least nine institutions for the amelioration of unfortunate and suffering humanity...."

To its alumni and educators the New York school is better known as Fanwood. In 1856 the school moved from its site on 50th Street in Manhattan to an estate in Washington Heights that overlooked the Hudson River.

Old cut of School's first permanent home on 50th Street and Fifth Avenue, New York City. The building was dedicated on September 30, 1829 and was enlarged three times before City's growth dictated School's removal to Washington Heights in 1856.

The estate had been the country home of Colonel James Monroe, a cousin of President Monroe, who had a small daughter named Fanny. The woods surrounding the Monroe house were knows as "Fanny's woods," and from this the estate became dubbed "Fanwood."*

The principal of the New York school, Dr. Harvey P. Peet, was a former associate of T.Gallaudet's father at the American School for the Deaf before going to New York. The two had held regular correspondence with each other after Dr. Peet left Hartford, and so Dr. Peet would know of T.Gallaudet's progress as a student at Trinity College. It is not surprising then that at a Board meeting, held on August 6, 1843, Dr. Peet made a motion that two new teachers, Samuel Porter (Yale M.A.), an experienced teacher, and T.Gallaudet be appointed to fill two vacancies. It was pointed out that both men were proficient in the use of the sign language. The motion was approved.

---

* From a publication put out for the school's sesquicentennial celebration in 1968.

When T.Gallaudet began his duties at the New York school he was listed on a roster of six professors. He was the only one with a B.A. degree; the others possessed M.A. degrees. His starting salary was $425 per annum plus room and board. Payments were made quarterly and for the first quarter he received $40 in cash.

T.Gallaudet's first class consisted of 10 boys and 10 girls, averaging 12 years in age. All were either born deaf or were deafened before the age of six, that is before they developed a language concept. All used natural gestures or signs as a means of conveying their wants or ideas in their homes. They had had no previous schooling before receiving instruction under T.Gallaudet. So it was first necessary to teach them to communicate with him and others in commonly used sign language. They were also given twice-a-week exercises in penmanship. With "Elementary Lessons" as a guide, the children acquired a vocabulary of many common words, some basic grammar, and when they could count to 100 they began to form sentences. Additionally, they learned short stories from the Holy Scriptures such as the creation, the flood, the ten commandments with brief biographical sketches of such characters as Abraham, Joseph, Moses, etc.

That T.Gallaudet became highly esteemed by the school children is evidenced by a testimonial of respect, printed without his knowledge, in the *New York Tribune*—and reprinted in *American Annals of the Deaf* in 1854 (vol. 6).

Mr. Gallaudet: The undersigned, pupils of the New York Institution for the Deaf and Dumb, entertaining a lively sense of the obligations which the deaf and dumb are under to you for your disinterested efforts in their behalf and for the uniform kindness which you have displayed during the long period of your connection with this institution as an instructor of the deaf and dumb as well as of the immense debt of gratitude which the deaf and dumb of this country owe to your honored father, the late Thomas H. Gallaudet, for the introduction of the present mode of educating the deaf and dumb; considering you as his proper representative and wishing to give some material evidence of our sentiments before we separate, some of us perhaps to meet no more on earth, we take this opportunity to present you a copy of Irving's and a copy of Shakespeare's works, with the hearfelt prayer that your life may long be spared to bless the deaf and dumb and that while you live you may enjoy all the happiness that is to be found on earth, and when death shall summon us from our labors we all may meet in Heaven.

(the names of 34 students, various classes, were printed here.)

Acknowledgment of Mr. Gallaudet.   Messrs. Trist, Morehouse, Chamberlayne and others—Gentlemen: As you have deemed it proper to make public the very kind address presented to me in connection with the elegant and highly acceptable testimonials of your esteem, allow me to publicly return to you my heartfelt thanks for the pleasing surprise which you and your associates so generously arranged for me. The whole scene of the presentation was one of the most affecting incidents of my life—one which memory will store away in her most cherished nook. May God's blessing ever rest upon you and all your deaf-mute friends, leading you through this life in the paths of wisdom and peace, and in the life to come, giving you an abundant entrance into the Heavenly Jerusalem, the City of our God. Thomas Gallaudet.

It is worthy of note here that when T.Gallaudet was ordained to the priesthood and began to minister to the deaf in areas beyond the Diocese of New York he had close relationships with many of the students who were signatories to the testimonial. For instance, James S. Wells served for many years as a layreader of the Mission at Grace Church in Baltimore, Md.; Mr. H. C. Rider, who married Helen Chandler—with T.Gallaudet officiating— was the founder and first editor of the *Deaf-Mutes' Journal*, first published in Mexico, N.Y., in 1871; John W. Chandler, brother of Helen, was the first president of the Empire State Association of the Deaf, which had its first convention in Syracuse, N.Y., on August 30, 1865; Thomas J. Trist was a member of an Executive Committee chosen in 1853 to forward the work of soliciting subscriptions for the erection of St. Ann's Church for the Deaf. More is said of these people in chapter four.

When T.Gallaudet accepted the professorship at the New York school he was still giving thought to preparing for the ministry and ordination in the Episcopal Church. Although he had been baptized in the Congregational Church during infancy he felt that he should again be baptized by a priest of the Episcopal Church. Soon after taking up residence in New York City he was baptized by the Rev. Dr. Forbes, rector of St. Luke's Church. He said afterwards in the Sketch—

> I caused sadness to my parents and suffered much mental pain myself for I showed my dissatisfaction with the Congregational system in which my dear parents had consecrated me as an infant to the loving service of our heavenly Father. I was so exercised as to the authority of the ministry that I could not find peace of mind till I had received Holy Baptism at the hands of a priest of the Church of God. As the years have rolled on my views have been modified and now I am satisfied that what is called lay baptism with water in the name of the Father and of the Son and of the Holy Ghost is valid. God grant that all who profess and call themselves Christians may soon be joined together in the unity of the historic Church founded upon Christ and his Apostles at the day of Pentecost, so that all perplexities as to the authority of the ministry and the validity of the sacraments may come to an end.

Soon after his baptism he was confirmed by Bishop Benjamin T. Onderdonk, who also received him as a candidate for Holy Orders.

In addition to teaching a class of 20 pupils, who had entered the school in September 1843 T.Gallaudet began his theological studies in his free time. On Sundays he taught Sunday School at St. Paul's Chapel in the city, and when it was his turn he conducted sign language services for the pupils in the school chapel.*

At this point in his life, quite unexpectedly, T.Gallaudet experienced the tender passion of love. Strangely, what took place was similar in some ways to what happened to his father years before—he fell in love with one of the

---

* In its 40th annual report the New York school made this statement: "School is opened and closed each day by the explanation of a portion of scripture, and by a prayer, in signs. Every Sunday two lectures or sermons, in the language of signs (the vernacular of our pupils), are delivered in the chapel by the President and the more experienced Professors, in rotation." And—"Such exercises are regularly, during the school term, held in our own and other American institutions." Indeed, in most residential schools for the deaf in the United States religious services and compulsory chapel attendance were common until the 1930s.

students at Hartford school, and married this young woman, Sophia Fowler, who became the mother of T.Gallaudet.

In his Sketch T.Gallaudet described the experience in this way—

> The disturbing element was my falling in love with Miss Elizabeth Budd, who had been elected by Dr. (Harvey Prindle) Peet, (Principal), as a member of his private class of deaf-mutes in the fall of 1843. I had determined, much as I loved and honored my silent mother, that I would not marry a deaf-mute, but the charms of this youthful beauty soon converted me. Our acquaintance ripened into intimacy and ere long we became engaged to be married, with the approval of the young lady's parents, Dr. and Mrs. B. W. Budd of New York City. My own parents thought I was too young to take such an important step but I could not help it. Results have shown that my wife and I were drawn to each other for a happy life.

This couple was married on July 15, 1845, at the Church of the Ascension in New York. A newspaper, the *New York Commercial Advertiser*, said it was an interesting affair because for 1 1/4 hours several hundreds of men, women, boys, girls and children, hearing or deaf, had been waiting for the bride and groom to appear. It was a very warm day and both the Rev. Dr. G. T. Bedell, rector and officiant— later becoming bishop of Ohio—and Dr. Peet, the bride's interpreter, chafed at the delay. Finally they came! "The groom, a fine young man of gentlemanly and intelligent aspect, the bride, a vision of beauty in her attire of snowy white, with the bridal chaplet crowning her fair brow."*

It is stated that on the honeymoon they paid a visit at the Perkins School for the Blind, Boston, to present his father's letter to Dr. Howe, its director. There they met Laura Bridgeman, the first deaf-blind person to complete the necessary education successfully. Laura took Mrs. Gallaudet's hand and asked, "How do you like your new husband?"

---

* From this account it appears that the groom arrived at the church with members of the wedding party—perhaps he had acted as an interpreter! But certainly the bride walked up the aisle on the arm of her father, Dr. Budd.

The newlyweds returned to New York City in early September, in time for T.Gallaudet to resume his duties as an instructor at the school. The couple made their home with Dr. Budd and his family at 22 Third Street. During this romantic interlude it appeared that T.Gallaudet forgot about his candidacy for holy orders. However, his ties with the Church were becoming stronger than ever. He became superintendent of the Sunday School at St. Stephen's parish church. Here Mrs. Budd and his wife Elizabeth were baptized, confirmed and received into communion with the Church. In the fall of 1845 he was received into membership with the New York Historical Society. Many prominent New Yorkers were members of this society, which held its meetings in the New York University Building on Washington Square. He also became a member of the New York Prison Discipline Society. And, of course, he continued to take turns with other teachers in conducting Sunday and weekday sign

STORY OF G. WASHINGTON & CHERRY TREE RETOLD

Professor Thomas Gallaudet had a favorite pupil, a little deaf-mute, who was unusually bright. At a gathering of teachers and educators T.Gallaudet asked the lad to tell the story of George Washington and the cherry tree. In sign language, with dramatic expressiveness and verve, the little fellow told the story. All went well until the father of George Washington came along and discovered the hacked-down cherry tree. The father then asked who had cut down his favorite cherry tree. At this point the story-teller transferred the hatchet to his left hand. The action surprised T.Gallaudet and, signalling to the boy to stop, he asked, "Where did you ever get the idea that George moved the hatchet to his left hand?" "Why," confidently responded the lad, "he needed his right hand to tell his father he had cut down the tree."—Philadelphia Ledger and reprinted in the *Deaf-Mutes' Journal* (Oct. 16, 1902).

services in the school chapel.

On May 9, 1848, a daughter was born to the T.Gallaudets. She was baptized at St. Stephen's and named Caroline Budd Gallaudet She would be the first of 7 children born to this family.

T.Gallaudet related that in the spring of 1849 he chanced to meet on the street a priest who inquired about his status as a candidate for holy orders. According to the Sketch this priest "put his right hand on my shoulder and told me pleasantly but firmly to go home and get my books out again, adding that if I chose I could be ready for my examinations in a year." T.Gallaudet considered that providential meeting to be one of the great turning points in his life.

Indeed, a year later he was examined for holy orders and recommended to the diocesan authorities for ordination. On Sunday, June 16, 1850, T.Gallaudet was ordained deacon by the Rt. Rev. Bishop Whittingham of Maryland at St. Stephen's Church. He then became assistant to the rector, the Rev. Dr. J. H. Price.

When T.Gallaudet returned from his summer vacation to his duties as a teacher at the New York school, and also his duties at St. Stephen's, he was impressed with the necessity of doing something to promote the spiritual welfare of the students after they left the institution and entered upon the battles of life. So in September 1850 he began a Bible class for them in the vestry room of St. Stephen's Church. In the Sketch he stated—

The class became too large for the place and we took a room on Bond Street. It was my privilege to baptize several adult deaf-mutes and in the spring of 1851 to present a class of eight deaf-mute women and men to be confirmed in St. Stephen's Church by the Rt. Rev Bishop Chase of New Hampshire. I interpreted the service and the bishop's address in the sign language.

On St. Peter's Day, June 29, 1851, T.Gallaudet was ordained to the priesthood in Grace Church, Brooklyn Heights. At this ceremony nine men were ordained deacons and nine, including T.Gallaudet, were ordained priests. The Bishop of Western New York, the Rt. Rev. Wm. H. Delancey, the officiant, reported that this was the largest ordination ever held in the United States. Those ordained were mostly graduates of General Theological Seminary, New York.

In the fall of 1851 T.Gallaudet left St. Stephen's to take charge of St. Paul's Chapel, Morrisania. This, added to his teaching duties at the school, put heavy responsibilities on his shoulders. Also, the death of his father, Thomas Hopkins Gallaudet, on September 10, 1851, and the birth of his second daughter, Virginia Butler, on October 2, made him conscious of the seriousness of life.

At this time an incident occurred that undoubtedly had a great influence on the course of his life. In his sketch he wrote—

> I became very much interested in Cornelia Lathrop, a lovely pupil of the Institution who had been seized with consumption and had gone to her home in New York City. I ministered to her as she gradually failed and gave her the Holy Communion. She grew wonderfully in spiritual life and I realized the privilege of being able to comfort and strengthen her by using the sign language. I officiated at the touching burial service and was led to the idea of founding a church in New York which should be the spiritual home of deaf-mutes.

Cornelia A. Lathrop became widely known in the Episcopal Church. According to the Rev. Guilbert C. Braddock, at one time vicar of St. Ann's Church for the Deaf, 1930-1945, a Sunday School book entitled "Cornelia; or the Deaf-Mute," first published in 1852 or 1853, was written by the Rt. Rev. Henry W. Lee, Bishop of Iowa, who had once lived in New York and was a friend of Cornelia's family. The Rev. Mr. Braddock stated that the story of Cornelia did for Church missions among the deaf what the story of Alice Cogswell did for the cause of the education of the deaf; it aroused sentiment in favor of all benevolent efforts to raise the deaf to the cultural status enjoyed by other people. He also wrote—

> This was, as we see now, a dispensation of Providence, for Cornelia's illness and confinement brought about a series of visits by the Rev. Thomas Gallaudet, son of Thomas Hopkins Gallaudet. In the course of these pastoral calls at the house of the Lathrops the young clergyman saw the great need of a

church for the deaf in which all the ministrations would be in the sign language. Through her mother's zeal, Cornelia had been baptized and confirmed in a church for the hearing, yet in her extremity only the sign language could convey to her the spiritual comforts of her religion.   The Rev. Mr. Gallaudet's prayers and discussions in the silent tongue sustained her until the day of her death, June 2nd, 1852, in her sixteenth year.   She was buried in Mt Hope Cemetery, Rochester, after a funeral service in St. Luke's Church, which is now the headquarters of the deaf mission in Rochester. Exactly four months after her death, on October 2nd, 1852, the Rev. Mr. Gallaudet established St. Ann's Church for the Deaf in New York City, which drew attention as the first institution of its kind in the world.[*]

T.Gallaudet, having resigned the work at Morrisania, held his opening services on the first Sunday in October 1852 in the small chapel of the New York University on Washington Square. The morning service was conducted by voice for the hearing and the afternoon in sign language for the deaf. He felt that the greatest good would be accomplished by associating the deaf with their hearing friends in a common parish life.   There were occasional combined services, both sets of people coming together and both languages used at the same time. However, the name of the church was to be St. Ann's Church for Deaf-Mutes[**]—the word "mute" would be dropped later. From friends, his family and neighboring parishes he secured much-needed funds and furnishings for the conduct of services of worship. Also, a building fund was started.

---

[*] The article on Cornelia Lathrop appeared under title "Notable Deaf Persons" in *The Frat* (Jan. 1941), a publication of the National Fraternal Association of the Deaf.

[**] The following statement with respect of the origin of the name is attributed to T.Gallaudet: "We desired one so that we could gracefully add to it the expression 'for Deaf-Mutes.' We learned that the early Church had commemorated the mother of the Virgin Mary under the title of Ann(a), and were quite content with that view of the subject, especially as the original meaning of the word is 'a gracious giver.'"—From "A Brief History of St. Ann's Church for the Deaf and its Founder, the Rev. Dr. Thomas Gallaudet," by the Rev. Eric Whiting, Vicar 1964-69.

During the five-year stay in the small chapel of the New York University quite a number of deaf persons were baptized, confirmed and admitted to Holy Communion in St. Ann's, which was incorporated and admitted into the convention of the Diocese of New York in 1854.

In 1857 St. Ann's was moved to the attractive lecture room of the new Historical Society Building on the southeast corner of Second Avenue and East 11th Street, having oral services morning and evening, and sign language services in the afternoon every Sunday. In his Sketch T.Gallaudet then wrote—

> In the Spring of 1858 a meeting of my friends was held in the hall where we worshipped. Bishop Potter presided. After several addresses it was decided that I ought to resign my position in the New York Institution for Deaf-Mutes and give myself more fully to St. Ann's Church. $1,000 for one year were subscribed toward my support and Mr. D. H. Haight offered me the position of tutor for his deaf-mute son, Henry J. Haight. I entered upon this new phase of my life October 1, 1858, having been for 15 years connected with the New York Institution for Deaf-Mutes.

So ended his official connection with the New York School, perhaps better known as Fanwood.

CHAPTER 4

St. Ann's Church For The Deaf

For those who know something of its history, St. Ann's Church for the Deaf New York City, evokes the name of the Rev. Thomas Gallaudet and vice versa. The ministry of T.Gallaudet was centered at St. Ann's, even though his ministry was almost nationwide—even reaching to European countries. He brought it forth and never abandoned it.

In the previous chapter the reader learns that this church came into being on the first Sunday of October, 1852, although it was without a house of worship of its own. The decision to have such a church building was made at a public meeting held on Thursday evening, March 3, 1853, in the small chapel of New York University. An account of this meeting was published in *American Annals of the Deaf* (vol. 5:169-181—1853). Presiding over the meeting, we learn, was the Right Rev. Dr. Wainwright, provisional bishop of the Diocese of New York. After he had opened the meeting with a prayer the Bishop "alluded to the large number of deaf-mutes in the city who are deprived of the ordinary access to the means of grace, and said that they had assembled to consider a plan which had been proposed, to offer to this class of persons the privilege of public worship in their own language of signs." He further remarked that "this idea of establishing a church for deaf-mutes was not an untried scheme, for the experiment had already been tried for five months in that very room with a truly encouraging result."

On motion of General Wetmore, seconded by Dr. Harvey P. Peet,* principal of the New York School for the Deaf, Professor Jacob Van Nostrand was appointed secretary of the meeting.

T.Gallaudet then came forward and spoke at considerable length on the rise and progress of education of the deaf in this country and the beginning and progress of his ministry in New York City. He stated, in part—

> At length the idea forced itself upon my mind that I ought to attempt to gather these persons around me in pastoral relations, and to establish for them a church. This idea gained strength from time to time, and having obtained the unanimous consent of the rectors of the different Episcopal churches in this city, I commenced holding the regular services of our church on the first Sunday of October, 1852, in this room in which we are now assembled. I have the morning service with the voice, that the parents, children, other relatives and friends of deaf-mutes may have the opportunity of joining with them in forming one parish. The afternoon I devote to the deaf-mutes, translating to them our service and preaching the same sermon which I use in the forenoon. The deaf-mutes have apparently taken great interest in this service, and have been present several times to the number of seventy and eighty.

It is then reported: "after his address, at the request of the bishop, and with a view of showing the definite and precise character of the sign-language, the Rev. Mr. Gallaudet translated the Creed, explaining the particular significance of each sign as he proceeded. After which he repeated it without interruption in the same way as he

---

* Harvey Prindel Peet, who was a member of the first graduating class of Yale College and served for nine years under the Rev. Thomas Hopkins Gallaudet as a teacher of the deaf at the American School for the Deaf, Hartford, Conn., became principal of the New York School for the Deaf (Fanwood) in 1831. He held the position for 36 years. He was succeeded by his son, Isaac Lewis Peet; his granddaughter, Elizabeth, became a prominent member of the Gallaudet University faculty, where she taught Romance languages and served as Dean of Women for nearly half a century (1910-51).—*The Gallaudet Alumnae.*

would do in divine service. There was quite a number of deaf-mutes present at this meeting, for the benefit of whom the Rev. Mr. Gallaudet reported the proceedings and speeches, in which they took a lively interest."

The following resolution was then made by Mr. Robert Gracie: "That a committee of twelve be appointed to counsel and assist the Rev. Mr. Gallaudet in carrying out the details of his undertaking." This was seconded by Gen. Wetmore.

Another resolution was made by Gen. J. Watson Webb, editor of the *Courier and Enquirer* as follows: "That the object brought before this meeting by the Rev. Thomas Gallaudet is one calculated to call forth the cordial encouragement and support of this community." This was seconded by Dr. Harvey P. Peet, president, or principal, of the New York School for the Deaf.

Dr. Peet then took the floor. At the conclusion of his address he stated: "Nearly thirty-six years ago the system of deaf-mute instruction was introduced into this country by the Rev. Thomas H. Gallaudet, who first employed the language of signs as the medium of devotion and of social and public worship. In every institution which has since been established this feature is embodied in its system of instruction. The son, following in the footsteps of the father, is the first to organize a church of the deaf and dumb, and institute a form of service conducted in this silent language addressed only to the eye. May it be his happiness and reward to know 'when the Lord writeth up the people, that this man was born there' (Ps. 87:6)."

The next resolution was then moved by the Rev. Dr. (Benjamin I.) Haight, professor in the Episcopal General Theological Seminary, as follows: "That St. Ann's Church for the Deaf-Mutes be commended to the favorable consideration of the clergy and laity of this city and vicinity, with the earnest expectation that its services may, ere long, be held in an appropriate edifice, consecrated to Almighty God."

Seconding the resolution was the Rev. G. T. Bedell, rector of the Church of the Ascension and, in 1873, consecrated Bishop of the Diocese of Ohio.

The minutes also state: "Mr. John Carlin, the

distinguished deaf-mute artist, delivered a brief address in the sign-language, which was translated by Prof. Bartlett. Mr. Carlin said that though he was a Presbyterian himself, yet he rejoiced in the privilege afforded him of public worship through the ministrations of the Rev. Mr. Gallaudet, and hoped that this movement might result in great good to all deaf-mutes."

At the conclusion of the meeting the resolutions were unanimously adopted and a committee of twelve was appointed by Bishop Wainwright.

Some interesting footnotes to this meeting are derived from the Parochial Register of St. Ann's; also *American Annals of the Deaf* (vol. 11) and *St. Ann's Bulletin.*

Under date of April 7, 1853, is a notation that Dr. (Harvey P.) Peet, the principal of the New York School for the Deaf, gave an exhibition of his pupils at Niblo's Garden in aid of the Building Fund of the church. Net proceeds amounted to $714.

On June 17th, the same year, the Rt. Rev. Bishop Wainwright confirmed in the chapel of New York University six deaf-mutes, one of whom was a young black man.

On the afternoon of October 9th the Rev. Francis J. Clerc, a deputy to the General Convention from Missouri, assisted T.Gallaudet at the service for the deaf-mutes and preached in the sign-language. It was a striking coincidence that the eldest sons of the two founders of the first permanent school for the deaf in America, that is, the Rev. Thomas Hopkins Gallaudet and Laurent Clerc, should be conducting a church service in the first church of christendom to undertake a special mission to deaf-mutes.

On December 1st, in the same room, there was "a large meeting of deaf-mutes favorable to helping forward this church movement." Mr. John Carlin presided and Mr. G. W. C. Gamage acted as secretary. "It appointed a deaf-mute collector who largely increased our building fund."

On December 25th (Christmas Day) St. Ann's used for the first time a 5–piece solid silver Communion set that had cost $150. The money was collected by Miss Jane Ward.

ACADEMY OF MUSIC,

Fourteenth Street.

GRAND CONCERT

With the Full Orchestra and Chorus of the ITALIAN OPERA,

VOLUNTEERED BY

Mlle. ELIZA VALENTINI

FOR THE

Building Fund of the Church for Deaf Mutes

The Rev. THOMAS GALLAUDET, Rector.

THURSDAY EVENING, May 22, 1856.

First appearance of Mrs. SHEEHAN, from Brooklyn,

Pupil of Mdlle. VALENTINI.

Recitations in the SIGN LANGUAGE, will be given by MR. G. C. W. GAMAGE, a DEAF-MUTE INSTRUCTOR, in the N. Y. Institution for the Deaf and Dumb. MR. I. L. PEET, Vice-Principal of the Institution, has kindly consented to interpret these Recitations.

PART I.

1. OVERTURE, Guillaume Tell,...........................ROSSINI.
2. RECITATION IN THE SIGN LANGUAGE,...........MR. GAMAGE.
3. GRAND AIR, De la Favorite,.........

PART II.

1. OVERTURE, Der Freyschutz,............................WEBER.
2. GRAND ARIA, from I Puritani,.......................BELLINI.
   Eliza Valentini.
3. "I NEVER CAN BE THINE," Ballad, Music composed by Mlle. VALENTINI
   Mme. De Lussan.
4. "THE BOUQUET de BAL," Ballad, Music composed by Mlle. VALENTINI.
   Mrs. Sheehan.
5. RECITATION IN THE SIGN LANGUAGE,............MR. GAMAGE.
6. BRINDISI, from Lucrezia Borgia,.....................DONIZETTI.
   Mrs. Sheehan.
7. The celebrated MARSEILLES HYMN, expressly arranged for this occasion, with full Orchestra and Chorus, will be sung and declamated by Eliza Valentini, with the French Flag.

Conductor of the Orchestra, - - MAX MARETZEK.

Who has generously volunteered his services, as well as all the others who sustain the principal parts.

Tickets 50 Cents, to all parts of the House.

For sale at the Hotels, Book, Drug and Music Stores; and also at the doors on the evening of the Concert.

Doors open at 7 o'clock. Concert to commence at 8.

The GRAND PIANO is from CHICKERING & SONS, 508 Broadway.

ELIZA VALENTINI'S Musical Compositions can be had at her rooms, No. 522 Broadway.

GEORGE F. NESBITT & CO. Printers, corner Pearl and Pine Streets, N. Y.

On September 11, 1854, St. Ann's was incorporated under the legal title of "The Rector, Church Wardens and Vestrymen of St. Ann's Church for Deaf-Mutes in the City of New York." T.Gallaudet was elected its Rector and "our parish was received into union with the Convention of the Diocese October 28th, 1854, at the special meeting which elected the Rev. Horatio Potter, D.D., Bishop of the Diocese." (On October 1st had occurred the death of Bishop Wainwright.)

On May 6, 1855, Bishop Potter visited St. Ann's for the first time and confirmed a class of 12, presented to him by the Rev. Thomas Gallaudet, Rector.

On August 10, 1855, the parish purchased four lots on the south side of 26th Street and east of Seventh Avenue for the sum of $16,500. These lots were freed of debt the following year, and in 1859 they were sold for $18,000. This provided most of the down payment for the 18th Street property that St. Ann's acquired that year.

* * *

In 1857, on November 1st, St. Ann's Parish moved from the facilities provided by New York University on Washington Square to the lecture room of the New York Historical Society on Second Avenue at 11th Street. This was at the suggestion of William Lewis Gallaudet, a brother of T.Gallaudet. But soon the congregation was to have its own home. This came about after T.Gallaudet had resigned from his teaching position at Fanwood—recorded in Chapter 3. In his Sketch he wrote—

> In the spring of 1859 a rumor reached us that the church and rectory in West 18th Street, near 5th Avenue, were for sale by the Baptist congregation who in 1858 had made an exchange of property with the Rector and Vestry of Christ Church. Negotiations were begun by the Wardens of St. Ann's Church, Messrs. G. R. Jackson and S. R. Comstock, aided by Mr. D. H. Haight, which resulted in our purchase of the property in July 1859 for $70,000. We were only able to pay $20,000, leaving $50,000 on bond and mortgage. After some alterations and repairs the first services were held on the first Sunday of August, 1859.... We felt thankful that we had made a good beginning.

Then in November of the same year the T.Gallaudet family moved into the rectory of this church, No. 9 West 18th Street, where, he said, "we lived for upwards of 35 years most happily and contentedly."

On Sunday, October 2, 1859, St. Ann's Church for the Deaf observed its seventh anniversary. An account of this, written up by T.Gallaudet, appeared in *American Annals of the Deaf* (vol 11). The statistics of the seven-year period were as follows: Baptized, infants, 57 (16

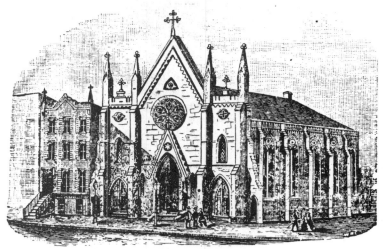

Old St. Ann's Church for the Deaf

children of deaf parents); adults, 18 (14 deaf). Confirmed, 43 (34 deaf). Married, 38 (14 deaf couples). Funerals, 42 (11 deaf). Communicants, about 110 (upwards of 50 deaf); reduced by death and removals to 90 (35 deaf). Fund for sick and poor, $626.13. Parish fund, $7,017.79. Building fund, nearly $21,000. The rector stated that he had performed several other baptisms, marriages and funeral services for deaf people prior to the formation of the parish and since its formation in other places, more or less distant from New York, so that, including all his ministerial labors among adult deaf persons and their families, the foregoing aggregates would be considerably increased. It was moreover stated that several of the deaf communicants had been confirmed in other churches.

T.Gallaudet also mentioned that at services in other cities during the year preceding the Seventh Anniversary he had acted as the interpreter for the deaf persons in attendance. The cities and churches mentioned were: St. Paul's Ch., Oxford; Christ Ch., Binghamton; St. John's Ch., Yonkers; and Christ Church, Hudson, New York; St. Paul's Ch., Hartford; Christ Ch. Guilford; and Trinity Ch., Southport, Connecticut; St. Paul's Ch., Boston; St. Stephen's Ch., Philadelphia; Grace Ch., Baltimore; Ch. of the Epiphany and St. John's Ch., Washington, D.C.

Some interesting notes regarding T.Gallaudet and his ministry to the deaf at St. Ann's were once made by his granddaughter, Mrs. Margaret Sherman Gillen as follows.

> His understanding of the deaf made him popular. Many of the pupils at Fanwood who had finished school and were going out in the world were gravitated to St. Ann's just to be near him—their friend and advisor. It is recorded that people of different faiths gathered there—Roman Catholics, Jews, Baptists and others—and it must be said that they did not know how to behave during sermons: they would gossip and call each other, and T.Gallaudet had to halt the service to admonish them. Slowly they learned from him to show reverence, even though they were not Episcopalians. He advised them to go to their own denominations for their spiritual needs, find sympathetic priests and rabbis who might learn the sign-language and then minster to them.

In an old copy of the *Deaf Mutes' Journal* (Oct. 26, 1882) this item is recorded: "Dr. Gallaudet made a scathing remark at one of his recent sermons. According to a reporter he said, 'People will think, judging from the number of mutes outside the church on the sidewalk, that the church is full and there is no room for them inside!'"

T.Gallaudet had close ties with his alma mater, Washington College at Hartford, Conn., and whenever possible he attended its commencement exercises. In 1845, the year the school changed its name to Trinity College, T.Gallaudet was awarded the degree of Master of Arts. From 1858 to 1864 he served as dean (president) of the alumni association.   At the school's 1862 commencement he delivered an oration on the subject, "Men of One Idea." At the same commencement he received the degree of S.T.D. (Doctor of Sacred Theology), which was later renamed Doctor of Divinity (D.D.). In 1869 his brother Edward M. also received an honorary L.L.D. degree from this college. In 1864 when Gallaudet University—originally named Columbia Institution for the Deaf & Dumb—was established by an edict of President Abraham Lincoln in Washington, D.C., Edward was named its president.

At St. Ann's Church were founded several organizations that ministered to the needy and deprived, such as the House for Old Men & Aged Couples, the Home for Incurables, the House of Mercy, the House of Rest for Consumptives. Although they operated independently of St. Ann's, T.Gallaudet served on their Board of Trustees or Managers.   He was also a member of the Executive Committee of the New York City Mission Society of the Episcopal Church, Diocese of New York, and meetings of this committee were held at St. Ann's; also, "the Alumni Association of the General Theological Seminary have had a number of their anniversaries here."

An organization of which T.Gallaudet was particularly proud was the Sisterhood of the Good Shepherd, over which he had a close and loving pastoral oversight for many years. In his Sketch he described the founding of this sisterhood as follows—

> On the second Tuesday after Easter, April 6th, 1869, at 12 noon, in St. Ann's Church, the Right Reverend Bishop Horatio Potter, D.D., founded the Sisterhood of the Good Shepherd and received Sisters Ellen, Serena and Elizabeth. The Right Reverend C. Doane, D.D., Bishop of Albany, preached the sermon. I was appointed the pastor. The sisters were in charge of St. Barnabas' House, belonging to the City Missions Society. I was a member of the Executive Committee. There was some opposition to entrusting the Sisterhood with this work. The Bishop thought I could harmonize matters though I was without experience in Sisterhood life. It was a new departure which led to most pleasant and profitable associations. This pastoral relation continued for many years. It was a great privilege to aid such

devoted women in their efforts to minister to poor women and children.

An organization that has continued to the present day was founded and incorporated in October 1872—The Church Mission to Deaf-Mutes. T.Gallaudet was appointed general manager. As a representative of this Society he pioneered Church work among the silent people throughout the greater part of the country. However, after a while he came to the conclusion that it was not expedient to maintain this Society as a general one. After a number of years the field which the Society cultivated was limited to the Dioceses of New York, Long Island, Newark, and Connecticut.

A very noteworthy project undertaken by the Society not long after its incorporation was the establishment of a Home for aged and infirm deaf people at 220 East 13th Street, New York, a rented house. Here lived nine people—four men and five women—under the care of the Matron, Miss Jane Middleton. This was the forerunner of the Gallaudet Home for Aged and Infirm Deaf-Mutes,* located on the Hudson River between Poughkeepsie and New Hamburg. The official opening was held on June 17, 1886 At that time it had 15 residents. The Gallaudet Home was always on T.Gallaudet's itinerary, and besides ministering to the old folks he personally oversaw and handled important matters pertaining to the Home. Since it was the only one of its kind in the country the Gallaudet Home admitted applicants from other states if room were available. T.Gallaudet also made it a strict policy to pass on applicants on a non-sectarian basis.

When the new Home at Poughkeepsie was opened for occupancy the building at 220 East 13th Street, was converted into the Mission House of the Church Mission to Deaf–Mutes under the charge of the Rev. Dr. Chamberlain and his wife. In 1887 it became the living quarters for the Rev. and Mrs. Anson T. Colt. The Rev. Mr.

---

* Bibliography: *History of the Gallaudet Home for Aged and Infirm Deaf-Mutes in the State of New York* by the Rev. Guilbert C. Braddock and printed on the occasion of the Fiftieth Anniversary of the Opening of the Home at Wappingers Falls, N.Y., 1936. Also *Gallaudet Alumni Bulletin*, vol. 3, no. 9.

Colt had been ordained to the priesthood in 1884. After learning the sign language he assisted T.Gallaudet with his ministry in the New England and New York states.

Another organization that had its birth at St. Ann's and of which T.Gallaudet was a sponsor is the Conference of Church Workers Among the Deaf (CCWAD). The proceedings of the meeting, held Tuesday and Wednesday, October 4-5, 1881, at St. Ann's, states that the Conference "opened with Morning Prayer and the celebration of the Holy Communion, Dr. Gallaudet officiating, assisted by Messrs. Chamberlain, Syle and Mann." The Rev. H. W. Syle, whose life and ministry has been written up in the supplement of this book, and the Rev. Austin Ward Mann, both deaf, were deacons. So also was another deaf man, the Rev. Job Turner. This national organization of Episcopal Church Workers continued to meet regularly through the years to the present time except for the period from 1913 to 1926. In 1970 its name was changed to the Episcopal Conference of the Deaf.[*] There will be mention of this organization again in later chapters.

In a report that was printed in the *American Annals of the Deaf* (vol. 8, 1856) T.Gallaudet said of services held in St. Ann's—"the morning being oral and in the afternoon in signs, in order that a self-supporting parish might be built up, composed not only of the persons for whose benefit it was specially started, but also of their children, other relatives and personal friends, possessed of all their faculties. It will be moreover recollected that in addition to these Sunday services, it was intended to do as much as possible toward cultivating the intellects of our deaf–mute brethren, improving their tastes, and, whenever necessary, caring for their temporal wants." He also described a Saturday evening lecture for the benefit of New York, as follows—

> On Saturday evening, February 11th, 1854, Prof. Laurent Clerc delivered a lecture to deaf–mutes in the university. This distinguished gentleman had so long been looked up to by his youthful companions in silence, as bearing a

---

[*] Bibliography: *Proceedings of the First American Conference on Church Work Among the Deaf*, Gallaudet University Archives.

prominent part in founding the first institution for their benefit in this country, that, upon this occasion, he was greeted by an unusually large assemblage of educated deaf-mutes desirous of showing their affection and esteem for this veteran instructor. He enchanted their attention for nearly two hours in a masterly manifestation of the graphic language of signs. He gave sketches of his visits to various cities, with him who has been styled the Father of deaf-mutes on these western shores (Thomas Hopkins Gallaudet), touching upon various interesting incidents connected with the important, though delicate, business of soliciting funds for the establishment of the American Asylum (school at Hartford, Conn.). He referred to various distinguished individuals with whom he came in contact during those times, stating that he had been honored with a seat at the right hand of Henry Clay, when the great Kentuckian was Speaker of the House of Representatives.

T.Gallaudet further stated—"Mr. (John) Carlin having expressed his great satisfaction at the pleasure which all had received from Mr. Clerc's address, and alluded encouragingly to the progress which had been made in collecting funds for the erection of the proposed church and lecture building, the meeting adjourned. This was considered one of the most interesting and satisfactory assemblies that had ever been held among deaf-mutes, giving evidence of the high degree of cultivation to which they had attained as respectable and useful members of society."

It can be seen from this report that St. Ann's congregation was composed of both hearing and deaf parishioners. Since T.Gallaudet was also frequently called upon to have services for the deaf in other cities—even as far away as Boston—or simply to officiate at weddings or funerals, it soon was necessary that he have an assistant at St. Ann's to take services when he was away. According to the Parochial Register of St. Ann's the first assistant minister to be appointed was the Rev. George Pennell, in September 1859. He resigned two years later. A succession of priests then acted as assistants to the rector.

At Epiphany, 1872, the Rev. Dr. John Chamberlain came to St. Ann's. He soon became proficient in sign-language communication, so that he could effectively minister to the deaf portion in the parish. Occasionally he accompanied T.Gallaudet on his trips to attend conventions or meetings of organizations of the deaf to do interpreting. He was a beloved pastor and served St. Ann's for nearly half a century—until his death in 1921 at the age of 82. Upon the retirement of T.Gallaudet in 1892 he became vicar of St. Ann's and general manager of the Church Mission to Deaf–Mutes.*

For upwards of ten years T.Gallaudet had held quarterly services for the deaf in Boston, mostly at the Chapel of the Good Shepherd, where the Rev. Edward H. Krans was pastor. The two priests became close friends, with the result that in 1874 the Rev. Mr. Krans accepted a call to become T.Gallaudet's assistant at St. Ann's, where as associate rector he would specially minister to the hearing and speaking portion of the parish and so allow T.Gallaudet to give still more time and attention to the Church Mission to Deaf–Mutes. Mr. Krans continued his association with St. Ann's until the church was relocated to 511 West 148th Street, Manhattan, in 1898. He then became rector of St. Matthew's Church in the city.

Despite the frequent absences of T.Gallaudet from St. Ann's, the church continued to grow. On the 25th anniversary of the parish—in 1877—he could report in his Sketch—

> During the 25 years of our parish life there were 1,294 persons baptized and 913 confirmed. The names of 1,275 communicants were placed on our list. There were 587 marriages and 761 burials. A large proportion of each classification were deaf–mutes and their relatives. There were received about $36,850 for charitable work in the parish, $16,645 for objects outside of the parish and $238,000 for the support of the Church, buying its property and paying for its improvements and repairs.... For several years much earnest work has been done for the sick and needy in our midst. In our chapel, besides the Sunday Schools, there have been a day–school, a sewing–school, a mothers'–meeting, and a social week–night gathering. All

---

* Bibliography: *A Missionary Chronicle*, Gallaudet U. Library. Also *The Deaf-Mutes' Journal* (Jan. 26, 1933).

this has finally crystallized into our Sisterhood and Brotherhood....

There were many personal and touching incidents in the life of T.Gallaudet that deserve mention. One of these is the death of his deaf mother, of which he wrote in his Sketch—

> In May 1877 my dear mother entered into the rest of Paradise to meet her husband and two beloved daughters, Jane, who died in 1853, and Sophia (Mrs. Hunter), who passed away in January 1865. The three were as fine characters as ever lived. Mother was almost translated. Apparently in perfect health on a Saturday evening, she retired to her room at my brother's (home) in Washington. Soon she was found kneeling at her bedside unconscious from apoplexy. She breathed through the night and experienced the great change on Lord's Day morning in the 80th year of her earthly silent pilgrimage.

The year 1887 being the year in which the 100th anniversary of the birth of T.Gallaudet's father would occur—on December 10th—a family gathering took place in Hartford on July 2nd as it was felt it would be impossible for them to assemble on the very day. In his Sketch he wrote— "....we drove about in a large omnibus. We saw the memorial window of old Center Church. We stood by the graves of the departed in the family plot of the beautiful Cedar Hill Cemetery. We enjoyed hospitality at the American Asylum for the Deaf and Dumb.... The next day we heard that our brother William Lewis Gallaudet (residing in Elizabeth, N.J.) had been taken to Paradise.... On the following Thursday some of the family were at the burial in the place we had so recently visited. I said the committal."

An event that must have given T.Gallaudet great joy to participate in took place at Gallaudet University on June 26, 1889. This was the unveiling of the bronze statue of his father giving a lesson to the little deaf girl Alice Cogswell, who inspired Thomas Hopkins Gallaudet to go to England and France to learn there how they were educating the deaf and then with the help of the deaf Frenchman Laurent Clerc establishing at Hartford the first permanent school for the deaf in America. T.Gallaudet said of it—"This

Dr. Thomas Hopkins Gallaudet, founder of American School for the Deaf at Hartford, Ct., in 1817.

Laurent Clerc, a deaf Frenchman who accompanied Dr. T. H. Gallaudet to America to help him establish the Hartford school.

Thomas Gallaudet as a young man

Photo by Alexander Pach

Elizabeth Budd Gallaudet, about the time of her marriage in 1845

Photo by Alexander Pach

Grandchildren of Thomas Gallaudet. Mrs. Margaret Gillen. at left, and Mrs. Eleanor Font. Both women were deaf. Photo by Alexander Pach.

Children and spouses of Thomas and Elizabeth Budd Gallaudet, taken about 1895. Left to right—Sarah Morse with her husband, the Rev. Richard Sherman, Jr.; Edith (a surviving twin); Virginia Butler; Alexander D. Shaw with wife Caroline Budd at his left; Dr. Bern Budd Gallaudet with spouse Eliza Elderkin, to the front of him; Elizabeth Fowler. From family photo album.

An interior view of the old St. Ann's Church at No. 9 West 18th Street, NYC.

Chancel of the new St. Ann's at 148th Street.

Edwin Allan Hodgson, for many years a vestryman of St. Ann's Church and for over 50 years editor of *The Deaf-Mutes' Journal*.

Gallaudet Home for Aged and Infirm Deaf-Mutes at Poughkeepsie, N.Y. A fire destroyed this home in 1900.

Thomas and Elizabeth Budd Gallaudet on the occasion of their golden wedding anniversary in 1895.

statue was one of Daniel C. French's most successful efforts. It was paid for by loving gifts of the silent people in every state and territory of the Union, a beautiful tribute to the memory of one of the best men that ever lived."

In 1891 a famous preacher, internationally renowned, the Rev. Phillips Brooks, D.D., was elected Bishop of the Diocese of Massachusetts. His fame apparently was well known to the deaf community, and when the Rev. S. Stanley Searing, assistant rector of the Church of the Good Shepherd in Boston, set up a reception for the deaf in the community to meet and greet the new bishop, the event was fully reported in the *Boston Herald* of October 16. The paper reported that "in all, 199 deaf-mutes were present." The Rev. Dr. Thomas Gallaudet was also present and, naturally, acted as the chief interpreter, as the Rev. Mr. Searing was not yet an accomplished sign-maker.—*The Deaf-Mutes Journal*, Oct. 22.

On March 14, 1892, T.Gallaudet attended the funeral of Bishop Gregory T. Bedell in the Church of the Ascension, New York. Before he went to Ohio he had been for many years a director of the New York School for the Deaf. T.Gallaudet and his wife were married in this church on July 15, 1845, by Bishop Bedell, who was then rector.

In the Sketch is this entry—"On June 3 (1892) I became three score and ten." And in that year, on October 2, St. Ann's commemorated the 40th anniversary of its founding. T.Gallaudet also wrote—"Being 70 years old and having been 40 years Rector of this church, I became, at my own request, accepted by the Vestry some time previous, Rector Emeritus. The Rev. Dr. Edward Krans became Rector. Time proved that this was a wise arrangement." The next day, October 3rd, "I had the great satisfaction of attending the laying of the cornerstone of the Church Mission House at the corner of 4th Avenue and 22nd Street."

All this time the city of New York was rapidly changing, and, of course, the changes effected the life of St. Ann's. In fact, it came about that this parish would leave its location at West 18th Street, near 5th Avenue, purchased in 1859 for the sum of $70,000. An editorial in the

November 1 issue of *The Deaf–Mutes' Journal* in 1894 conveyed this information to the readership—

> St. Ann's Church for Deaf–Mutes has been sold to a syndicate for $192,000. It is more than likely that the new church will be situated on the upper west side of the city, which is the best location for it. The center of the deaf–mute population is above 80th Street, and St. Ann's at present is right in the heart of the business district....

In due course of time the purchasers of the 18th Street property took the buildings entirely down. No trace of them is left and large business structures have risen in their place. One, according to T.Gallaudet's Sketch, was called *St. Ann's.*

• • •

A CRISIS AT ST. ANN'S

Reprinted from A Missionary Chronicle, *Year 1897*

The year 1897 was a critical year in the history of St. Ann's Church for the Deaf in New York City. In fact, it nearly went out of existence.

With the sale of the old church building on West 18th Street in 1894 the deaf people of the city felt deprived of a house of worship, although the Church of St. John the Evangelist on West 11th Street had been placed at their disposal. Then it was proposed that St. Ann's consolidate with a parish known as St. Matthew's—and that all the money obtained from the sale of St. Ann's. amounting to, then, over $200,000 be turned over to St. Matthew's. More, the consolidated church would be known as St. Matthew's!

In a two–column editorial in the April 8 issue of the *Deaf-Mutes' Journal,* Mr. E. A. Hodgson, editor, who for many years had been on the vestry of St. Ann's Church for the Deaf, asserted in no uncertain terms that the deaf parishioners were being defrauded—given the short end of the stick. A reprint of an article appearing in the *New York Advertiser* stated that "Mr. H. Comer, senior warden and the eldest vestryman of the church, who objected to the proposed consolidation," had sent in a letter of resignation from the vestry. Another report stated that Mr. Comer recently was elected treasurer of the endowment fund, and that an examination of the books showed up a loss of $17,000.

At another meeting of the vestry held one evening at the Church of St. John the Evangelist to resolve the consolidation matter. Mr. Comer is reported to have termed the action of the hearing members of St. Ann's Church—by voting affirmatively for the proposal— "Robbery! Downright robbery!" Even the Rev. Dr. Gallaudet, who was present in the capacity of an interpreter, was blamed for failing to make the motion voted upon clear to the deaf and siding with the Rev. Dr Krans, who would share the office of rector with the appointed priest of St. Matthew's when the action of the vestry took effect. Mr. Hodgson also complained that in regard to this meeting, "it appears that pains were taken to have the hearing members present, while few of the deaf were aware of it as only about fifty were present."

However, a few months later—in 1898—a new St. Ann's came into being. This, no doubt, was in large measure due to Mr. Hodgson's determined opposition to actions taken by hearing members of the vestry. (4-8 & 6-24).

Plans for a New St. Ann's

The aftermath of the vestry vote upon the consolidation of St. Ann's Church for the Deaf with St. Matthew's parish in New York City is best understood in the statements made in an editorial appearing in the March 3 issue of the *DMJ*, as follows:

> A few of the more prominent deaf gentlemen interested in "St. Ann's Church for Deaf–Mutes" were invited to inspect a rough draft of the architect's plans for a new church edifice for deaf–mutes exclusively. The plans were exhibited at St. Matthew's Church on Monday evening, February 28.
>
> It is understood that the endowment fund for "St. Ann's Church for Deaf–Mutes" was placed under control of the

officers of St. Matthew's on the same evening. The "endowment fund" trustees held a short session previous to the showing of the architect's drawings.

From Rev. Dr. Gallaudet we get the information that the five lots on 148th and 149th Streets, between Amsterdam Avenue and the Boulevard, constitute the appropriation for the building of the church for deaf-mutes. The idea is to sell three of these lots, retaining two of them as the site for the church, and using money obtained from the sale to erect the building.

The lots originally cost $36,000, and are probably worth at the present time about $40,000. Therefore, taking the estimate as a basis, there will be $24,000 available for building the church.

These five lots were purchased with money acquired from the sale of the old "St. Ann's Church for Deaf-Mutes" on 18th Street.

The balance of the money turned over to St. Matthew's Church by "consolidation" will be more than $156,000. But St. Matthew's agrees to be responsible for any monetary obligations that the deaf-mute church cannot meet.

The new church is to be adapted in every respect to the needs of a deaf congregation, and will have an inclined floor and plenty of light from overhead. Space has been reserved for a parish building, but there will be a well-lighted basement to the church which can be used for meeting purposes. (3-3)

Construction on the new church was rapid, as the DMJ reported that on Sunday afternoon, December 4 of 1898 "about a hundred and twenty-five of the deaf attended the initial services in the new St. Ann's Church.... The day was rainy and the wind blowing a gale, and had it not been for these conditions there would surely have been double that number. Rev. Dr. Gallaudet, who apparently has recovered from his late attack of rheumatism and is in his 75th year, did not like to go out on such a day, but he could not miss it, and braved the storm."

The sermon was preached orally by the Rev. Dr. Gallaudet, Rev. Dr. Chamberlain interpreting. Among other things, Dr. Gallaudet announced that he was vicar of the new church and that Dr. Chamberlain was his assistant. (12–8).

The new St. Ann's was consecrated by the Right Rev.

Henry C. Potter, Bishop of New York, on St. Stephen's Day, Monday, December 26, in impressive ceremonies, beginning at 11 o'clock in the morning. The Rev. Dr. Gallaudet, the vicar, and the Rev. Dr. Chamberlain, curate, were assisted by the Rev. Dr. True and the Rev. Mr. Homans, and also these deaf missionaries: The Rev. Messrs. J. M. Koehler, Charles O. Dantzer, Austin W. Mann, James H. Cloud, and Oliver J. Whildin. Assistant to the Bishop was the Rev. Dr. Krans, rector of St. Matthew's Church. Fully 200 people were present, of whom most were deaf. (12-29).

This church edifice remained the spiritual center of the Episcopalian deaf people and their friends in the New York area until it was closed down in the year 1949.[*]

---

[*] Although the church at West 148th Street closed down in 1949 it did not lose its corporate identity. St. Ann's Church for the Deaf continues to be a mission affiliated with the Diocese of New York.

CHAPTER 5

Outreach

B y her outreach to deaf people everywhere St. Ann's Church for the Deaf, New York City, became, in many ways, their "mother church," and through the ministry of her pastor, the Rev. Dr. Thomas Gallaudet—dubbed the Apostle to the Deaf—many blessings came to them.   T.Gallaudet was concerned not only with the quality of their spiritual life but also their intellectual, vocational and social attainments.

It must puzzle some readers how T.Gallaudet could continue his work as chief pastor of St. Ann's while carrying on such a far-reaching ministry in other areas throughout the country.   He himself was at times concerned about this as he wrote in his Sketch: "I was often absent in the missions to deaf-mutes in other cities, being criticized by some for neglecting the church of which I was Rector, but the Lord watched over us and kept us from failure."

One of T.Gallaudet's assignments, relating to the education of the deaf, was to examine the classes at the schools for the deaf located at Flint, Mich., and Faribault,

Minn.—in addition to his responsibility, as a director, at the New York School for the Deaf. In his trips to these western states he would arrange for holding services for the deaf in churches near the schools, as is evident by a letter he wrote to Bishop Henry B. Whipple of Minnesota from Washington, D.C., and dated May 26, 1869.[*] T.Gallaudet wrote as follows—

Washington, D.C.
May 24, 1869

My Dear Bishop Whipple,

I expect to hold a service for Deaf-Mutes in Albany on Sunday, June 20th. By continuous travel, can I reach Faribault on time for the Consecration of the Church on Thursday, the 24th?

Can I then probably get back to Flint, Michigan, by the following Saturday night or early Sunday morning?

If I should get to Faribault, could I have a short service for Deaf–Mutes in this newly consecrated Church at some hour of the afternoon or evening—I think Mr. Noyes would let the pupils attend such a service.

Hoping that God, in his good providence will allow me to be with you at the consecration of the Church, so dear to your heart heart (sic.), I am.

Yours Sincerely,
Thomas Gallaudet.

Please address me - No. 9 W. 18th St. N.Y.

I am off on a deaf-mute expedition to Washington, Baltimore & Philadelphia.

Will there be any passes or half-fares issued, say from Milwaukee or Chicago westward.

I am going to Flint to conduct the closing examination of the Inst. for the Deaf & Dumb & will have my expenses paid to that point & back to New York.

---

[*] This letter has been preserved by the Archives/Manuscripts Division of the Minnesota Historical Society at St. Paul. Their permission has been given to reprint the text of the letter here.

In New York State T.Gallaudet had a hand in the establishment of three schools for the deaf—at Rome (1875), Rochester (1876) and Malone (1884). In fact, in recent editions of *American Annals of the Deaf* he is listed as one of the founders of the Rome School for the Deaf—in addition to Alphonso Johnson and 81 Rome, N.Y., citizens. T.Gallaudet favored the creation of more smaller schools for the deaf rather than the enlargement of a single school to accommodate an increasing enrollment. He felt that the deaf pupils should not be too far away from their homes for the week-end's sojourn.

At a memorial service held in St. Luke's Church, Rochester, N.Y., following the death of T.Gallaudet in 1902, one of the speakers was Dr. Zenas F. Westervelt, LL.D., who is credited by the *American Annals of the Deaf* as being the founder of the school for the deaf at Rochester. Dr. Westervelt had this to say with regard to the beginnings of the Rochester school:

> Those of you who attended our school in its first years, 20 to 27 years ago, will recall Dr. Gallaudet's frequent visits. You, perhaps, do not remember, however, that he was one of the incorporators, and for many, one of its trustees. He made a special journey to Rochester to attend the meeting that was called to consider the establishing of this institution, and gave the friends who were interested in this movement, the benefit of his knowledge and experience.... In 1876, at the time of our incorporation, and for a number of years afterward, Dr. Gallaudet's church work brought him quite regularly to Rochester. But later he attended meetings of our Board—with considerable inconvenience, and finally his increasing duties in New York led him to withdraw from the Board. However, from time to time, as he was able, he visited the school and inspected its works, with the interest of a teacher of experience and one of the founders of the school.
> —*The Deaf-Mutes' Journal* (Nov. 13, 1902).

Another school for the deaf in New York State that T.Gallaudet helped to bring into existence—in 1884—was the Northern New York Institution at Malone.   The founder and first principal of this school actually was Mr.

Henry C. Rider, who was a graduate of the New York School for the Deaf and afterwards became the publisher and editor of the *Deaf-Mutes' Journal* at Mexico, N.Y. When Mr. Rider first attempted to establish the school at Malone he was met with determined opposition from the State Board of Charities. But with the help of T.Gallaudet this opposition was overcome and the school was opened with 27 pupils. Mr. Rider served as principal until 1896, when he was succeeded by his son, Mr. Edward C. Rider. This school, however was closed down in 1943.[*]

It was not only in New York that T.Gallaudet had a hand in the establishment of schools for the deaf. While attending the 11th biennial convention of the New England Gallaudet Association of Deaf-Mutes in Salem, Mass,. on February 22-23, 1876, he was approached by William B. Swett with the idea of the establishment of an industrial home and school for destitute adult deaf. As expected T.Gallaudet readily supported it, which idea was then brought up at a meeting and approved. T.Gallaudet then was appointed chairman of the committee to set up the home and school with Mr. Swett taking charge of soliciting funds for the project. This Home and school was established in Beverly, Mass., in 1880, with T.Gallaudet elected as president of the Board of Trustees and Mr. Swett, who was deaf, named its first superintendent. However, the idea of the home was discarded in favor of the school, which later became the Beverly School for the Deaf.

T.Gallaudet is known to have given assistance to a young deaf man who started a day school for the deaf in Scranton, Pa., in 1880. This deaf man, Mr. Jacob Koehler, is believed to have received encouragement and support for this project by another deaf man, the Rev. Henry Winter Syle of Philadelphia, the first deaf man to receive holy orders in the Christian Church. Later Mr. Koehler became a licensed lay missionary in the Diocese of Central Pennsylvania and then was enrolled as a special student at the Divinity School in Philadelphia during the

---

[*] Bibliography: *American Annals of the Deaf* (vol. 58—1913). Also *Malone Evening Telegram* (Mar. 23, 1934. Micro., N.Y. State Lib., Albany).

WOMAN ANNOYS DR. GALLAUDET

Reprinted from the *Deaf-Mutes' Journal*, June, 1887

New York City.—"Dr. Gallaudet, the pastor of St. Ann's Church for Deaf-Mutes, caused the arrest yesterday of Catherine Hall, a middle-aged woman, who has been a source of annoyance to him for many years.

"Ten years ago a child of Mrs. Hall was taken away from her care because she was not a proper person to take care of it, and, through the medium of Dr. Gallaudet, a good home was procured for the lad out West. Since that time the woman has been engaged in giving Dr. Gallaudet much trouble and annoyance. She has disturbed the services in his church many times and has annoyed him at his home. He has had her arrested thirteen times within the past ten years.

"Recently she has been going about among the doctor's neighbors carrying a large stone under her apron and threatened him with death. For his own protection he was compelled to have her arrested again. Dr. Willard Parker accompanied the pastor to Jefferson Market Police Court and told Justice Ford that he did not think the woman was in her right mind. Justice Ford committed her to the Island for a year."

1885-86 academic year. In 1887 he was ordained to the priesthood. More will be said of the Rev. Mr. Koehler and the Rev. Mr. Syle in the next chapter and in the Supplement of this book.

Another school started by a deaf man—Mr. Lars M. Larson—in 1887, was the New Mexico School for the Deaf at Santa Fe. The school at first consisted of only five pupils and was located in Mr. Larson's home. In 1886 T.Gallaudet accompanied by a deaf priest, the Rev. Austin Ward Mann, and Mrs Mann, visited Santa Fe. These two priests had an unusual service there in the Church of the Holy Faith. It was reported in the Santa Fe newspaper that during the service the two priests gave entirely different sermons simultaneously—one in sign language, the other vocally with spoken words! Whether it was due to this publicity or not, the next year Mr. Larson received an appropriation from the Territorial Legislature and moved his school into a larger building that had once been the residence of an Episcopal bishop.*

The ministry of T.Gallaudet seems all-encompassing, touching all areas of the lives of the deaf people in this country. On these pages only some aspects or illustrations of this can be shown. He is credited, indirectly at least, with the establishment of the Empire State Association of the Deaf, considered the first of these state associations. Its first convention was held in Syracuse on August 30, 1865.** In *A Brief History of the E.S.A.D.* by the Rev. Guilbert C. Braddock, at one time vicar of St. Ann's, it is stated—

> For the immediate background of the founding of the E.S.A.D., we have to look to the little town of Mexico, or Mexicoville, Oswego County, about halfway between Syracuse and Watertown. In this locality lived a country squire, John Wilkes Chandler, of the Class of 1857, New York Institution for the Deaf, and Helen, his deaf sister, Class of 1853. Soon after school days they were joined by a schoolmate, Henry C. Rider, Class of 1855, who married Helen Chandler and settled down to do business in Mexico. John Chandler was also married to a deaf woman, Josephine Grace Colvin, from Lewiston, Niagra County, Class of 1852 or so. These two families, intelligent, widely known, and hospitable, became the nucleus of visitors, and their village

---

* Bibliography: *The Deaf Churchman* (vol. 46, no. 1, Gallaudet U. Lib.).

** The deaf people of New York probably were challenged to start their own organization when it was known that the New England Gallaudet Association—named for Thomas Hopkins Gallaudet—had come into being, with T.Gallaudet its "advisor." Also the Fanwood School alumni had their first reunion in 1851 in New York City; they probably saw then the desirablility of having a state-wide organization. It is believed that because of John Chandler's frail health the leaders felt that the convention should be held in the small town of Syracuse rather than New York City.—Henry Buzzard.

became the chief social center of upstate deaf. As early as 1861 the weekly newspaper of Mexico reported a great gathering of the deaf at the Chandler and Rider homes on December 12: twenty-five persons coming by buckboard and pony from the counties of Jefferson, Cayuga, Onondaga and Oswego to meet together and attend church services conducted by the Rev. Thomas Gallaudet   This was undoubtedly the germ of the movement which culminated in the forming of the Association.

This history states that both the Rev. Dr. Gallaudet and Dr. Isaac Peet, principal of the New York School for the Deaf, were present at the first convention to act as interpreters and "give some pointers" when needed. In the proceedings of the 7th convention of the E.S.A.D. it was stated: "The Rev. Dr. Gallaudet has attended every convention since the organization of this Society and has rendered us material assistance, not only while acting as an interpreter between ourselves and the hearing people present, but has also in many ways added much to the interest of the meetings and to the enjoyment of those in attendance."

Still another organization of the deaf that came into being—in 1881—with T.Gallaudet's participation and support was the Pennsylvania Society for the Advancement of the Deaf (PSAD). The meetings were held August 24-27 in the Senate Chamber of the Capitol at Harrisburg. Also present was the Rev. Dr. Francis J. Clerc, who played an important role in the ministry to the deaf in Pennsylvania. Both were elected honorary members of this organization, which at first was known as the Pennsylvania Deaf-Mute Association. No doubt the interpreting skills of both men were in great demand as addresses were made by Governor Hoyt and Ex-Governor Curtin of Pennsylvania; Mayor Herman of Harrisburg; W. A. Lindsey Deputy Superintendent of Public Instruction, and the Rev. Job Turner, a deaf man who had been ordained to the diaconate a year before. T.Gallaudet and Dr. Clerc themselves made addresses. The keynote speaker, however, was Mr. John Carlin, the oldest alumnus of the Pennsylvania school at Philadelphia and a well-known artist.* A sponsor who did much to promote this convention was the Rev. H. W. Syle, mentioned above in connection with the establishment of the day school for the deaf at Scranton. The Rev. Mr. Syle was elected first president of this new organization. One of the outcomes of the creation of the P.S.A.D. was the establishment of a home for aged and infirm deaf persons at Doylestown in 1901. The Home is still in existence, though it is now known as the George W. Nevil Home, which is located in the Philadelphia area.

---

* A short sketch of the life of John Carlin will be found in the Appendix of this book.

CHAPTER 6

The Deaf Receive Holy Orders

As T.Gallaudet extended his ministry outward from St. Ann's Church for the Deaf and New York City it became clear to him that he would need a small army of assistants—preferably men in holy orders who could relate easily to the deaf—to carry on the ministry to the deaf that he had started up in the various metropolitan areas he had visited. The extent of his travels and missionary activity on behalf of the deaf is vividly revealed in the following news item that appeared in the June 3, 1875, issue of the *Deaf-Mutes' Journal:*

ALBANY, N.Y.—On Sunday, April 25, at 2 p.m., Rev. Dr. Gallaudet held the service for deaf-mutes in St. Paul's Church, Albany. . . . On Monday evening, April 26, Rev. Dr. Gallaudet was at Burlington, Vermont, and in St. Paul's Church he addressed the congregation in relation to the Church Mission to the Deaf-Mutes. On the following Tuesday afternoon he stopped at Granville to consult with Mr. Berry about future work, and the next day he was busy in Albany; and after having become satisfied that the legislation was complete in relation to the Central New York Institution for the Deaf (at Rome) and explained the matter to Gov. (Samuel J.) Tilden personally, he reached New York in the evening in time to marry at the Rectory Mr. Patrick Fanning and Miss Carrie A. Waldruff, both deaf-mutes. The next evening he was in Philadelphia and married at the residence of the bride's parents, Mr. Washington Houston, graduate of the New York Institution, and Miss Hanna E. Franks of Pennsylvania Institution. At midnight Dr. Gallaudet left Philadelphia and, via Williamsport, Elmira, and Canandaigua, reached Rochester the next day. On the following Sunday forenoon several deaf-mutes were confirmed by Bishop Coxe in St. Luke's Church, Rev. Dr. Gallaudet interpreting. In the afternoon Dr. Gallaudet held in the same church a service for deaf-mutes. This associate mission located in Rochester is under the charge of Mr. J. C. Acker, ably and kindly assisted by Mr. Edward P. Hart. . . . Dr. Gallaudet was to hold a service for deaf-mutes in Boston last Sunday, and if nothing interferes with his plans, he will also hold one in Mexico, N.Y., on Sunday afternoon, the 30th inst., at 3 o'clock.

T.Gallaudet did persuade several hearing persons to aspire to this ministry. A few already have been mentioned in previous chapters. One of the most notable was the Rev. Dr. John Chamberlain, T.Gallaudet's assistant at St. Ann's in New York City; others provided a part-time ministry elsewhere—the Rev. Dr. Francis J. Clerc in Pennsylvania, the Rev. Thomas B. Berry in upper New York State (also in Wisconsin and South Dakota, where he established the school for the deaf at Sioux Falls), the Rev. S. Stanley Searing in Massachusetts, and the Rev. Anson T. Colt in Brooklyn, N.Y.*

Heretofore no deaf man had ever received ordination in the Christian Church, though there were a number of deaf lay leaders and missionaries, particularly in the New England states, where Christian churches considered ordination unnecessary and probably even frivolous.

By a happy circumstance there appeared in the Church a singularly gifted and well-educated deaf man by the name of Henry Winter Syle, who began his collegiate education at Trinity College, Hartford, in 1863—the college from

---

* Bibliography: Introductory Chapter 5, *A Missionary Chronicle*, Gallaudet University Library.

which T.Gallaudet graduated in 1842. In 1869, after having studied at St. John's College of Cambridge University, England, Mr. Syle accepted a professorship at the New York School for the Deaf. Whether the idea of entering the ministry arose in the mind of Mr. Syle or was conceived by T.Gallaudet in not known with certainty. At any rate, when Mr. Syle moved to Philadelphia in 1875 and there took employment as an assayer in the United States Government mint, he was admitted a candidate for holy orders in the Diocese of Pennsylvania, and on October 8, 1876, at St. Stephen's Church in Philadelphia, Mr. Syle was ordained to the diaconate by the Rt. Rev. William Bacon Stevens, Fifth Bishop of Pennsylvania—despite some objections to this by clergy who believed that deafness, by itself, disqualified any person from receiving holy orders in the Church. It is believed that Mr. Syle is the first deaf-mute to be ordained in Christendom.

In his sermon at Mr. Syle's ordination, interpreted by T.Gallaudet, Bishop Stevens pointed out that the deaf were disqualified by neither the Bible nor the canons of the Church. By way of example he referred to St. Luke's account of Zacharias, "a priest of the course of Abia, after he was smitten speechless, did not cease to officiate because he was dumb, and depart at once to his own house, but he remained serving in the temple until the days of his ministration were ended."

With regard to Church canons, Bishop Stevens had this to say; "Others have asked, 'Do not the ancient canons forbid such an ordination?' Again I answer No. The only one of the canons of the early councils which at all speak of this class is the 78th of the Primitive Canons, commonly called 'Apostolical.' This says, 'If one is totally deaf or blind let him not be made a Bishop; not that he is thus defiled, but that the affairs of the Church may not be hindered'; or, as Bingham translates the last clause, 'because he will not be able to perform the duties of his function.' "*

---

* Bibliography: Bishop Stevens' sermon, in toto, is printed in *The Deaf Churchman* (vol. 35, no.2--1959); the ordination of H.W.Syle, *The Deaf-Mutes' Journal* (11-30—1876).

That this ordination of Henry Winter Syle opened the door to other deaf men aspiring to receive holy orders in the Church is evident, for just a few weeks later—on January 25, 1877—Mr. Austin Ward Mann, who had held a professorship at the Michigan School for the Deaf at Flint, was ordained a deacon in Grace Church, Cleveland, Ohio, by the Rt. Rev. Bishop G. T. Bedell, who, while rector of the Church of the Ascension in New York City, had married T.Gallaudet and Elizabeth Budd in 1845. (Bishop Bedell was also a director of the New York School for the Deaf.) It was T.Gallaudet who acted as interpreter for Mr. Mann when he was being examined prior to his ordination, then again at the ordination. The Rev. Mr. Mann had been licensed by the Bishop of Michigan in 1875 to serve as a lay missionary in the midwest states. But evidently the Diocese of Michigan declined to confer holy orders upon him because there was no precedent for so doing in the case of a deaf man.

Following the ordination of the Rev. Mr. Mann by three years a third deaf man was made a deacon at St. Paul's Church, Richmond, Va., on January 17, 1880, by the Rt. Rev. Bishop Francis M. Whittle. This man—Mr. Job Turner, who was a little over the age of 59—had been for many years a teacher at the school for the deaf at Staunton. Mr. Turner had been presented for confirmation at Worcester, Mass., in the year 1877 by T.Gallaudet, and it was T.Gallaudet who preached the sermon at the ordination ceremony in St. Paul's Church. T.Gallaudet was also present at the Rev. Mr. Turner's ordination to the priesthood, which took place June 26, 1891, in the chapel of the Episcopal Theological Seminary in Virginia at Alexandria.

In the year 1883, during the 34th General Convention of the Church, held in Philadelphia, the two deaf men first made deacons were raised to the priesthood at an ordination service held October 14 in the Church of the Covenant. A very detailed account of the ceremony appeared in the *Philadelphia Inquirer* dated October 15. Excerpts of this newspaper story follow—

The church was well filled when the exercises began.... after Hymn 153 had been sung, Rev. Thomas Gallaudet, D.D., of

New York, who was to preach the sermon, was introduced....
Rev. Mr. John Chamberlain of Iowa (an assistant at St. Ann's,
N.Y.C.) stood up in the chancel as Dr. Gallaudet began his
sermon, and interpreted the sermon to the deaf-mutes, who
sat in a body near the front of the chancel. Dr. Gallaudet
sketched the progress of deaf-mute education from the
establishment of the first school in Hartford, by this father,
in 1817.   As illustrating the individuality of the
sign-language, he mentioned that while he was in Brussels
in August last he preached to a congregation of about twenty
deaf-mutes—English, French and Belgian—and his sign
language was comprehended perfectly by all. "Sounds," he
said, "are only outward symbols of ideas, just as signs are."

At the conclusion of the sermon, Rev. Henry W. Syle and
Rev. Austin W. Mann were presented for ordination.... Sitting
within the chancel, one at each end of the communion table
(altar), were Bishop William B. Stevens (of Pennsylvania) and
Bishop Gregory T. Bedell, of Ohio, while nine other
clergymen surrounded them.   Among them the placid
countenance and venerable form of .i.Rev. Edward William
Syle;,* father of one of the candidates, was especially
noticeable.

Bishop Stevens read the exhortation, and it was
interpreted by Dr. Gallaudet to the two candidates, who stood
in their robes at the chancel rail. Eagerly did they watch the
motions of the reverend gentleman as he conveyed to them
the words the bishop was speaking. The bishop then asked
Mr. Syle the questions laid down in the Prayer Book. As Dr.
Gallaudet finished interpreting each question Mr. Syle
handed a slip of paper, on which was written his answer, to
Rev. Mr. Clerc of Phillipsburg, who read it aloud.

Rev. Mr. Mann then arose, and Bishop Bedell stated the
questions, and answers would be interpreted. He asked the
same questions asked by Bishop Stevens, and Mr. Mann
slowly communicated his answers, using only his right hand
in replying. The ceremony of laying on of hands was then
performed, Bishop Stevens and several others laying their
hands on Mr. Syle's head, and Bishop Bedell performing that
office for Mr. Mann.

---

* The father of the deaf ordinand Syle, the Rev. Dr. Edward William
Syle, was Professor of History and Moral Theology in the Imperial
University of Japan. Previously, he was a missionary in China, where
his son was born November 6, 1846. A childhood disease deprived him of
his hearing at the age of six, and the loss of voice gradually followed.

The sacrament of the Lord's Supper was then administered to the newly ordained priests and they were welcomed within the chancel rail. A special invitation was given to the deaf-mutes to commune immediately after the clergy, and there were enough present to occupy the long chancel rail twice. The sacrament was then administered to the congregation, and the audience was dismissed with the benediction by Bishop Bedell.

Following the ordination service in the Church of the Covenant the clergy ministering to the deaf moved to St. Stephen's Church to begin the second meeting of the Conference of Church Workers Among the Deaf. The Rev. Dr. Francis J. Clerc, son of the deaf teacher Laurent Clerc and rector of St. Paul's Church, Phillipsburg, was elected president and the Rev. Mr. Syle was chosen secretary and treasurer. Before closing the meeting with a service of Evening Prayer the missioners voted to accept the invitation of the Rev. Mr. Mann, one of the newly ordained priests, to hold the next biennial meeting in his home city of Cleveland in 1885. All three Philadelphia newspapers—the *Times*, the *Inquirer* and the *Evening Telegram*—gave lengthy and appreciative coverage to this meeting. The *Deaf-Mutes' Journal* reprinted excerpts of the story in the *Philadelphia Times*.

● ● ●

During the lifetime of T.Gallaudet six more more deaf men were ordained priests in the Church. All were graduates of Gallaudet University except the Rev. J. M. Koehler, who left the institution before he had finished the course. It must have pleased T.Gallaudet to realize that his younger brother, Edward Miner Gallaudet, became the founder and first president of a school that was providing for these deaf men a basic liberal arts education that qualified them, educationally, to become candidates for holy orders. What is remarkable is that T.Gallaudet was able to participate in the ordination services of all these six except two—the Rev. J. H. Cloud, ordained to the priesthood in St. Louis, Mo., and the Rev. Harry Van Allen, who was ordained a priest just a few months before the death of T.Gallaudet in 1902.

The Rev. Jacob M. Koehler (1860-1932), ordained a priest in 1887, was born in York, Pa., on July 4, 1860. He lost his hearing at the age of 12 years after an attack of spinal meningitis. His father was the principal of a private school and provided for him an excellent preliminary education, which he completed with two years at the Pennsylvania School for the Deaf in Philadelphia. In 1877 he entered the preparatory class of Gallaudet University. In 1879 he left college to establish a school for the deaf in Scranton, Pa. In 1881 he resigned his position as principal of the school over disagreement about method of teaching and became itinerant missionary to the deaf in the Diocese of Central Pennsylvania.

Mr. Koehler was the first deaf man admitted to a theological seminary as a student. He commenced the course at the Divinity School in Philadelphia in 1882. He was ordained a deacon on June 13, 1886, at St. James' Church, Lancaster, Pa., and made a priest on November 2, 1887, at Christ Church, Reading, Pa. Among the clergy present on both occasions were T.Gallaudet and the Rev. H. W. Syle, the founder and first vicar of All Souls' Church for the Deaf, Philadelphia. Upon the death of the Rev. Mr. Syle in 1890 the Rev. Mr. Koehler was called to this church to serve as vicar. He continued as missionary in the other dioceses of Pennsylvania; also in Delaware, New Jersey and Maryland. In 1903 he retired temporarily from Church work and spent several years on commercial work. Opportunity to serve the Church came to him again in 1909, when he was appointed missionary in the Sixth and Seventh Provinces (the northwest and southwest states, from Minnesota to Arizona).

The Rev. Mr. Koehler was an honorary Master of Arts at Gallaudet University, and a past president of the National Association of the Deaf (1896-1900), the Pennsylvania Society for the Advancement of the Deaf and the Conference of Church Workers Among the Deaf. He represented America at the World Congress of the Deaf in Paris in 1889, and made three other trips to Europe. He had a knowledge of German, French and Dutch. To the younger clergy he was a commanding figure, a dignified personification of the voice of experience in all matters connected with the education and evangelization of the deaf.[*]

•   •   •

The Rev. James Henry Cloud (1862-1926) was born in Chambersburg, Ind., on April 26, 1862. His hearing was impaired at the age of seven years, but he continued his education in the public schools until the age of 14. He then continued his education at the Illinois School for the Deaf and at Gallaudet University, from which he graduated in 1886. During his senior year he established a Bible class for the deaf at the Church of the Ascension, Washington, D.C. So notable were his efforts in this connection that he was awarded the Bishop Pinkney Scholarship for a course at Seabury Divinity School; but he declined it, preferring to earn his own living without further delay.   He undertook studies for the ministry privately, in the midst of his duties at the Illinois school, and in 1889 was ordained deacon at Trinity Church, Jacksonville, Ill.   In the same year he received his Master's degree from Gallaudet University.   For a short time he was an assistant at All Souls' Church for the Deaf, Philadelphia, of which the Rev. Mr. Koehler was then vicar.   In the autumn of the year 1890 he accepted appointment as principal of the new public school for the deaf—the Gallaudet School for the Deaf—in St. Louis, Mo. He was to hold this position until near the close of his life. At the same time he persisted in his Church work.   He was elevated to the priesthood in January 1893. He was the priest-in-charge of St. Thomas' Mission for the Deaf in St. Louis and doing as much mission work as possible in the Sixth and Seventh Provinces as an auxiliary to the Rev. Austin Ward Mann, general missionary to the deaf in the north central sates.   For a time (1909-1917) he was

---

[*] Bibliography: *The Silent Missionary*,, Sept., 1936.

assisted in this immense field of operations by the Rev. J. M. Koehler and restricted his own efforts to St. Thomas' Mission. He was awarded an honorary Doctor's degree by Gallaudet University in 1914. Dr. Cloud was known as the "fighting president" of the National Association of the Deaf from 1917 to 1923. He was renowned as a lecturer as well as a preacher.

● ● ●

The Rev. Charles Orvis Dantzer (1864-1924). T. Gallaudet, in his Sketch, wrote of this man: "Having previously examined Mr. C. Orvis Dantzer, a candidate for orders in the Diocese of Central New York under Bishop F. D. Huntington, I was present at his ordination as deacon in Grace Church, Syracuse, on the 10th of March (1892). I preached the sermon and bade the youthful minister God-speed in his mission to deaf-mutes in the Dioceses of Central and Western New York."

The Rev. Mr. Dantzer was born in Buffalo, N.Y., on September 19, 1864. He became deaf at the age of 8. Mr. Dantzer was awarded both a Bachelor's and Master's degree by Gallaudet University. After his ordination to the priesthood in 1895 the Rev. Mr. Dantzer served as a missioner in the Diocese of Central New York from 1891 until June 1, 1904, when he was appointed vicar of All Souls' Church for the Deaf, Philadelphia. There, with the help of Mrs. Margaret Syle, widow of the Rev. H. W. Syle who died in 1890, he built the new All Souls' Church for the Deaf that was consecrated on December 20, 1913. He was loved by his parishioners and at his death October 26, 1924, the layreader, James S. Reider, said of him:

> The late C. O. Dantzer had an easy, clear, and pleasing command of the sign-language, which made him easily understood in the pulpit, on the platform, and in conversation.   His preaching was earnest, instructive, helpful, and inspiring, rather than brilliant, probably so from a natural desire to adapt to all hearers. Even then at times he was singularly eloquent and impressive in driving home the teachings of the scriptures. There was nothing showy in

his style of sign delivery, no unnecessary flourishes, but it was uniformly graceful as the sign-language is intended to be.

•　•　•

The Rev. Oliver John Whildin (1869-1943) had the distinction of being born at sea—October 22, 1869. His parents settled in Lansford, Pa., near Hazelton. At the age of six he became totally deaf but retained his power of speech, which enabled him to attend the public school of Lansford until his 12th year. Later he went to Gallaudet University, graduating in 1892. In Philadelphia he met the Rev. J. M. Koehler, then vicar of All Souls' Church for the Deaf. Soon afterwards he was enrolled as a student at the Divinity School in Philadelphia and while pursuing his studies he took charge of the deaf-mute mission at Grace Church, Baltimore Md., as a missioner. When he was ordained a deacon at All Souls' Church for the Deaf in 1898 T.Gallaudet delivered the sermon. He was raised to the priesthood in the same church in 1901, and at that time another deaf man—Franklin C. Smielau, a recent graduate of the Divinity School—was ordained a deacon. The Bishop of Iowa ordained the Rev. Mr. Whildin and the Bishop of Central Pennsylvania ordained Mr. Smielau. T.Gallaudet interpreted the sermon and his assistant, the Rev. Dr. John Chamberlain, interpreted other parts of the service.

The Rev. Mr. Whildin was the founder of missions in Maryland, Virginia, North Carolina and West Virginia, where he had an important role in the building of St. Elizabeth's Church for the Deaf at Wheeling. He had much to do with re-activating the Conference of Church Workers Among the Deaf, which had last met in 1913. At a convention held in Philadelphia in 1926—the 15th—16 deaf missioners came together to work for the strengthening and extension of the ministry. Only two were absent, one because of illness. The Rev. Mr. Whildin was the presiding officer and he served as president of the organization until 1937. He also gave the CCWAD its official publication, *The Silent Missionary,* * which began in 1924 as a mimeographed news-letter. During his ministry the Rev. Mr. Whildin was instrumental in the creation of two endowment funds of the CCWAD (now called the Episcopal Conference of the Deaf). These funds, the Morrill Fund and the Fleming Fund, provide for the ECD substantial income for the ministry to the deaf.

●   ●   ●

The Rev. Harry John Van Allen (1867-1919) was general missionary in the Dioceses of Albany, Central New York and Western New York. In 1895 he was appointed lay missionary and four years later he was ordained a deacon by the Rt. Rev. Bishop W. C. Doane in St. Paul's Church, Albany. He was advanced to the priesthood by the same bishop February 20, 1902.

Just a few weeks before his death on April 17, 1919, the Rev. Mr. Van Allen had been honored at a special service held in St. Paul's Church, Albany, to commemorate his 25th year in missionary work with the deaf. One of the speakers at this event, at which more than 100 deaf people from far and near were assembled, was the Rev. Dr. Edgar A. Enos, rector of St. Paul's Church, Troy, N.Y. Dr. Enos' words are recorded in a front-page article in the *Deaf-Mutes' Journal* (March 6). A few excerpts from this article are given here as follows—

He praised highly the efficient way in which the work had been carried on under Mr. Van Allen's direction, and he paid

---

* A paper called the *Silent Missionary* was first published in Philadelphia in 1886 in behalf of the Missions to the Deaf in the Dioceses of Pennsylvania, Central Pennsylvania, New Jersey, Delaware and Maryland. The Rev. H. W. Syle was editor and the Rev. J. M. Koehler was associate editor. The 16 pages were printed from moveable type. Upon the death of the Rev. Mr. Syle in 1890 the Rev. Mr. Koehler became editor. But it seems this paper ceased publication in 1892. The Volta Bureau has in its library in Washington, D.C., a bound set of these papers. Also, photo-copies are in the repository of the Gallaudet University Archives.

high tribute to Mr. Van Allen's faithfulness, self-sacrifice and devotion, and to his intellectual endowments—especially his ability to express his thoughts in direct and fluent English.... In addition he has acted as secretary to the Joint Committee of Advice for Church Workers Among the Deaf since 1907, a position which has brought him into contact with most of the bishops of the American Church....

An interesting sidelight to the life of the Rev Mr. Van Allen, as it relates to his ministry, is a news item printed in the January 1899 issue of the *Silent Worker* (published at the New Jersey School for the Deaf, Trenton) that was sent in by the Washington correspondent, Mrs. C. C. Colby. It stated that in the spring of 1886 a Gallaudet College (now University) senior by the name of Robert S. Lyons, from Ireland, organized a Bible class for adult deaf residents of Washington at Ascension Church The class had four teachers in succession before it was finally discontinued. "Two of the teachers," she said, "have since entered the (ordained) ministry of the Episcopal Church—Rev. J. H. Cloud (St. Louis, Mo.) and Rev. H. Van Allen (Central New York)."

●   ●   ●

The Rev. Franklin Charles Smielau (1875-1940), who was born August 27, 1875, in Cincinnati, Ohio, was a missionary in the western Pennsylvania dioceses and when the Rev. C. O. Dantzer was appointed vicar of All Souls' Church for the Deaf, Philadelphia, he extended his missionary activities to western New York (1904-1916). Before his retirement in 1933 he was general missionary in the state of Ohio. Having lost his hearing at the age of seven, he attended a day school for three years, then entered the school for the deaf at Columbus, graduating in 1892, valedictorian of his class. Afterwards he went to Gallaudet University, graduating in 1897—again as valedictorian of his class. He received his theological education at the Divinity School in Philadelphia—he even took the course in Hebrew according to a biographer. He was ordained to the diaconate at All Souls' Church for the Deaf in 1901 at the same service that the Rev. Mr. Whildin (above) was made a priest. Then in 1902 he was ordained a priest in the Cathedral Church of the Nativity, South Bethlehem, Pa. The Rt. Rev. Bishop Ethelbert Talbot was the officiant and the Rev. J. M. Koehler was the presenter.

"Smike," as he was known to his colleagues, was considered an outstanding "sign-language orator." He was credited by the deaf people of Pennsylvania with removing the restriction against their operating motor vehicles. With regard to this there appeared in the *Harrisburg Telegraph* in March of 1924 this editorial comment.

> Arrangements for a committee of deaf persons, Rev. Franklin C. Smielau, chairman, Selinsgrove, Prof. J. A. McIlvaine, Mt. Airy (Philadelphia), and Frank A. Leitner, Wilkinsburg, to assist Paul D. Wright, State Highway Commissioner, in making regulations for the operation of motor vehicles by deaf persons is one of the unique things undertaken by highway officials in the great task of looking after more than a million cars and their drivers.... and there are some deaf-mutes who can run a car much better than some people with normal facilities.

●   ●   ●

Much of the material in this chapter has come from *A Missionary Chronicle*, published in 1984. Including the Rev. Henry W. Syle, forty-four deaf men—and one deaf woman—have been ordained priests in the Episcopal Church. It is noteworthy that this woman, the Rev. Virginia Nagel, who was made a priest in 1988, was ordained in the same church that the Rev. Mr. Syle was made a deacon on October 8, 1876, that is, St. Stephen's Church, Philadelphia. It also may be of interest that 32 of these priests received their education at Gallaudet University.

CHAPTER 7

Missionary Journeys

T he Rev. Dr. Thomas Gallaudet was an indefatigable
traveler all his life and this was during a period
when train travel, for instance, was comparatively
primitive: trains were slow and dusty and without such
comforts as air conditioning, which modern-day travelers
take for granted. However, train travel must have been at
little cost to him for he held passes given him by the
railway lines he used, or was given a substantial discount,
as were also most ordained clergymen. Also, as can be
seen by the letter T.Gallaudet wrote to Bishop Whipple of
Minnesota (chapter 5), he was reimbursed for rail travel
by some schools for the deaf which invited him to evaluate
their graduates at the end of the school year—Michigan,
Minnesota, Ohio, and the schools in New York State.
Furthermore, on business for the Church Mission to
Deaf-Mutes he, of course, as General Manager, had his

travel expenses paid by that organization. When he attended conventions of educators of the deaf he usually went as a delegate from Fanwood since he was a member of the school's board of directors. T.Gallaudet never knowingly complained of problems or hardships associated with his travels.

It was not until he resigned from his position as a professor at the New York School for the Deaf—Fanwood— in 1858 that he was free to take extended trips for the promotion of Church work amongst the deaf. However, it is known that even before he resigned from the teaching work he accepted invitations to hold services for the deaf elsewhere than in New York City. For instance, it was reported by Mr. J. P. Marsh, the leader of the Deaf-Mutes' Bible Class in Boston, that "Mr. T.Gallaudet, one of the instructors of the N.Y. Institution, offered his services to my Bible class for a Sabbath in November, 1855. He was gladly invited to preach, and our meeting was fully attended by the class with much pleasure."[*]

It was not until 1859 that T.Gallaudet began his extended missionary journeys that took him away from New York City for several days at a time. The first of these was to Baltimore, Md. An account of this visit and the first service for the deaf there is graphically set forth in a sermon delivered by the Rev. Arthur C. Powell, rector of Grace Church on the occasion of a celebration of the 40th anniversary of the deaf-mute mission in Baltimore, held on the evenings of March 2nd and 3rd, 1899, in Grace Church. This sermon was printed in toto in the March 1899 issue of the Silent Worker. Excerpts are printed below.

> In the year 1858 a wealthy gentleman of New York invited Dr. Gallaudet to become a tutor of his son, who was a deaf-mute, and offered him $400 for such services. At the same time other friends assured him $1,000 per annum if he would resign his position as teacher (in the New York School

---

[*] The full report of Mr. Marsh was printed in *American Annals of the Deaf* (1857). An account of the life of Jonathan P. Marsh and the beginning of the Bible class in Boston was printed in the April 1942 issue of *The Frat* under title of "Notable Deaf Persons" by the Rev. Guilbert C. Braddock, at one time vicar of St. Ann's Church for the Deaf in New York.

for the Deaf) and devote himself more wholly to work among the deaf and dumb. He accepted both offers. Very soon thereafter Mr. Haight requested him to take his son on a pleasure trip to Philadelphia, Baltimore and Washington. At once it occurred to him that this would be a good opportunity to inaugurate services in these important cities for the benefit of that class to which his life was now to be devoted. When a resident of Hartford he had been on very kindly terms with the Rev. Dr. Arthur Cleveland Coxe, who was then rector of St. John's Church. Dr. Coxe has since been elected rector of Grace Church, Baltimore. To him Dr. Gallaudet at once wrote his desires; and from him he received a most cordial invitation to use Grace Church for any service he might desire. So Dr. Gallaudet came immediately hither, with his young pupil, reaching this city on Friday, February 25th, 1859. They stopped at Barnum's Hotel. Speedily they made their way, through a blinding snow storm which prevailed all day, to the residence of Dr. Coxe on Madison St.; but found that he was out of the city, though he had left assurances that he would be back in time for the evening service. Dr. Gallaudet did not know any of the deaf-mutes of Baltimore, but as he was passing Mt. Calvary Church he met a policeman and made his plans known to him. The officer happened to know a deaf-mute and directed him to his home in the western part of the city. Going thither he found a deaf-mute named William Workington, working at his carpenter's bench in an attic. Both he and his wife were deaf-mutes. The Doctor urged Mr. Workington to go at once to all his friends and announce to them that a special service would be held that evening in Grace Church. This he did, while the Dr. and his companion returned to the hotel. In the evening he made his way to the church "through a violent, driving snow storm"—as he describes it—and to his delight found the rector there to greet him, and also his assistant, the Rev. Mr. Easton. There were 19 deaf-mutes in the church and eight other persons. It was estimated that there were 100 mutes in Baltimore at that time. The service was conducted by the Rev. Dr. Coxe and his assistant, with the Rev. Dr. Gallaudet interpreting it for the benefit of the deaf-mutes, in the sign-language. Dr. Gallaudet then made an address, the first ever made to the deaf of Baltimore, in which he outlined his plans and asked their co-operation. The Rev. Dr. Coxe added his warm approval of the plan, and placed Grace Church at the disposal of the deaf-mutes. From that day to this it has been their religious home.

Not mentioned in the above is T.Gallaudet's visit to Washington D.C., on the week-end following. In an account of the history of St. Barnabas' Mission of the Deaf, Washington, D.C., the Rev. Guilbert C. Braddock stated: "The first church service for the deaf in the Capital City of the Nation was held by the Rev. Thomas Gallaudet on February 27th, 1859, in St. John's Church (near the White House), six deaf persons being present among the hearing congregation...." Also, it is of interest to note that in the Monday, February 28th edition of the *Washington Evening Star* appeared the names of T.Gallaudet and his traveling companion H. J. Haight—already mentioned in this chapter—as being guests at the "Willards' Hotel." (It was the practice of this newspaper to print the names of guests staying in the city hotels.)

Among those present at the service in Grace Church, Baltimore, on Friday evening probably was a deaf man named Samuel A. Adams, who was a teacher in the School for the Colored Deaf and Blind, then located in Baltimore City. Mr. Adams, the first deaf layreader on record, offered his aid in establishing a permanent mission in Baltimore.

Only a week later—on March 4—T.Gallaudet visited Philadelphia, and there, at St. Stephen's Church, he planted the seed that was to produce All Souls' Church for the Deaf. An account of this is given in a history of All Souls' Church for the Deaf, Philadelphia, published by the Pennsylvania Diocesan Commission on Church Work Among the Deaf during the episcopate of the Rt. Rev. Bishop O. W. Whitaker and the pastorate of the Rev. Charles O. Dantzer. It is reprinted in the appendix of this book.

In the year 1864 T.Gallaudet visited Chicago and there, at St. James' Church, he held a service for the deaf. A vivid account of this was given in an old periodical, the *Northwestern Church*, dated May 26, 1864. Fifty-one years later—on October 2, 1915—All Angels' Church for the Deaf was consecrated by Bishop Charles P. Anderson and with the Rev. George F. Flick as pastor.

Not a long afterwards—in 1869—T.Gallaudet was at Faribault, Minn. An account of this visit appeared on the editorial page of the *Central Republican* of Faribault on June 23rd, 1869; it describes a "Church Service for Deaf-Mutes" held in the Cathedral of Our Merciful Saviour on the preceding Sunday. Dr. Gallaudet first gave a 15-minute talk in sign-language for the benefit of the deaf people present—without using his voice. Then he delivered another address for the audience in general, which was interpreted by Professor Noyes (of the Minnesota School for the Deaf).

In 1877 T.Gallaudet made the first of several missionary journeys with the Rev. Austin Ward Mann a deaf man who had been ordained to the diaconate January 25 in Grace Church, Cleveland, Ohio, that year. The journey began at Pittsburgh on June 10 with visits to Trinity Church and the new school for the deaf at Turtle Creek. The two then proceeded west through Ohio—with stops at Delaware, Columbus, Dayton and Cincinnati—and Kentucky (Newport and Louisville), then Indianapolis, and ending at Cleveland on June 22, on which day T.Gallaudet returned to New York, going via Pittsburgh and Philadelphia. Schools also were visited in Ohio, Kentucky and Indiana. (Reported in the July 5th issue of the *Deaf-Mutes' Journal.*)

The following year, in the early part of January, the two again embarked on a missionary journey that began on the 15th in Detroit, Mich., took them as far south as St. Louis, Mo,. and ended at Cleveland, Ohio, on the 25th, being the Feast of the Conversion of St. Paul and also the first anniversary of Mr. Mann's ordination to the diaconate. The two not only had services for the deaf but visited the University of Michigan at Ann Arbor and a deaf man in a prison in Jackson. Enroute to Detroit T.Gallaudet had made stops in Mexico, Geneva and Buffalo, N.Y.

An account of this journey was written up for the *Deaf-Mutes' Journal* dated February 2nd. In the Appendix is printed the Rev. Mr. Mann's "10th Annual report of Church Work Among Deaf-Mutes in the Central Western and North Western Dioceses."

In the same year—on February 6th—the ministry to the deaf was started in Newark, N. J., at St. John's Church by T.Gallaudet and the rector, the Rev. Dr. G. C. Pennell, who had previously had association with T.Gallaudet in the ministry while serving as Archdeacon of the Convocation of Ogdensburg in northern New York.

A missionary journey of seven weeks duration was undertaken in 1879 by T.Gallaudet in company with a deaf man who was a lay missionary and did not receive holy orders, as a deacon, until the following year at the age of 59. This man, Mr. Job Turner, had met T.Gallaudet two years before at a service in Worcester, Mass., where he was confirmed the next day by Bishop Paddock and then was immediately given a license to act as a layreader in conducting services for the deaf in Massachusetts and other New England states.*

The following account of the journey of the two comes from the letters that Mr. Turner wrote to the *Deaf-Mutes' Journal* from different localities in the South.

On January 7, 1879, Professor Job Turner and the Rev. Dr. Thomas Gallaudet met in Baltimore and began a missionary journey that took them through ten southern states. They visited as many schools for the deaf, where they sometimes had informal services in churches in the cities where the schools were located, also large population centers.

Cities visited were Frederick, Md., Romney, W. Va., Staunton, Va., and Richmond, where "we called on Governor Holliday of Virginia. He spelt out 'Glad to see you.' He can spell on the fingers as we do."

From Richmond they proceeded to Petersburg, Va., where they had a special service in Grace Church before going on to Raleigh, N.C., where the two dined with Governor Vance and Superintendent Gudger and his teachers. Mr. Turner said of their visit to the North Carolina Institution for Colored Deaf, Dumb, and Blind: "I gave a little colored girl two words, man and bird, requesting her to write them into a sentence, and

---

* After spending six months in New England Mr. Turner moved to Virginia and with Staunton as his headquarters became a "missionary-at-large," a term given him by his colleagues. In 1880 he was ordained a deacon in St Paul's Church, Richmond, Va., and in 1891 he was raised to the priesthood in the chapel of Virginia Theological Seminary, Alexandria, Va. Like T.Gallaudet, he was an indefatigable traveler; besides his nation-wide travels in the United States he made trips to such places as Mexico, Canada, Cuba and Europe. Mr. Turner was older than T.Gallaudet by two years and outlived him by one year.

she introduced them into a sentence by writing: "A man shoots a bird.'"

Next they went to Cedar Spring, S.C., where they visited the School for the Deaf and Blind, and had an evening service for the deaf in a Spartanburg church. They also visited the grave of the founder of the school, the Rev. N. P. Walker.

The next stop was at Athens, where Dr. Gallaudet was invited to address the students of the University of Georgia. He also had an evening service in this city and, on the evening of January 26, in St. Phillip's Church, Atlanta.

From Atlanta they went on to Knoxville, Tenn. Here "Mr. Ijams (the principal of the school) and ourselves took dinner with the Rev. Mr. Duncan today, and Rev. Dr. Humes, the president of the University of Tennessee, was with us. It was truly a very pleasant time. Tonight there will be a service for deaf-mutes and others in St. John's Church, one of the prettiest churches that I ever saw."

Then they were guests of Superintendent Connor of the Georgia Institution for the Deaf and Dumb at Cave Spring. Mr. Turner stated that to John J. Flournoy, a deaf-mute of Georgia, belongs the credit of establishing an institution for the education of deaf-mutes..... The school was opened in a log cabin May 15, 1846.

Mr. Turner's next letter is addressed from Talladega, Ala., and dated Feb. 1. Two days later they were in Montgomery, "one of the most attractive cities of the South." They accompanied Dr. Johnson, superintendent of the school at Talladega, to the Capitol, where he spoke before a legislative committee. And they were introduced to Governor Cobbs.

The missionaries next went to Mobile, Ala., then to Jackson, Miss. Dr. Gallaudet himself wrote from New Orleans, where they had services one Sunday morning. The next day they departed for Savannah, Ga., a 36-hour train trip. Then on to Charleston, S.C., Wilmington, N.C., and Norfolk, where they had a service in Christ Church, and from where they departed by boat to Baltimore. Dr. Gallaudet returned at once to New York, arriving in time to have services at St. Ann's on Sunday, February 23.

The last extended missionary journey of T.Gallaudet—a noteworthy one—was made in 1886 in company with the Rev. and Mrs. Austin Ward Mann. Mr. Mann planned the scheduled stopovers where the two missionaries would hold church services enroute from Cleveland, Ohio, to San Francisco, Calif.*

He also notified newspapers of their plans so that reporters could be present at the services and write up stories for their papers. When there was a write-up in one of the papers Mr. Mann sent clippings to the *Deaf-Mutes' Journal* in New York for reprinting. These reprints furnish readers with a great deal of information about the two missionaries and the services held by them. Also, in *The Spirit of Missions* (vol. 61,no.8—Aug. 1896) he wrote of this visit to the west coast: "In the summer of 1886, while attending a national convention of instructors of the deaf at Berkeley, California, I held the first Prayer Book service in the sign language on the Pacific coast, at Trinity Church, San Francisco." Mr. Mann's schedule of appointments, printed in the Journal, must have been in itself an ambitious exercise for 14 cities are listed for visiting from June 27 to July 30. The schedule does not include Los Angeles, probably because plans to visit this city could not be made at the time the copy had to be given to the Journal printer. Mr. Mann's schedule of appointments is reprinted here.

June 27.........Cleveland, O., 10:30 a.m., Trinity Church.
                Cleveland, O., 8:30 p.m., Grace Church.
June 28.........Indianapolis, Ind., 7:30 p.m., Christ Church.
June 29.........St. Louis, Mo,, 7:00 p.m., Christ Church.
June 30.........Kansas City, 7:00 p.m., Grace Church.
July 1...........Topeka, 7;30 p.m., Grace Cathedral.
July 4...........Denver, 10:30 a.m., The Cathedral.
                Denver, 3:00 p.m., The Cathedral.
                Denver, 5:00 p.m., Emmanuel Church.
                Denver, 7:30 p.m., Trinity Memorial Church.
July 5...........Denver, 7:30 p.m.,Church to be announced.
July 6...........Colorado Springs, 7:30 p.m., Grace Church.
July 7...........Manitou, 7:30 p.m., St.Andrew's Church.

---

* At Berkeley, across the Bay from San Francisco, was held the 11th convention of American Instructors of the Deaf and Dumb July 14-16, hosted by the State of California at the California School for the Deaf.

July 8...........Pueblo, 7:30 p.m., St. Peter's Church.
July 11.........Salt Lake City, 10:30 a.m., St. Mark's
               Cathedral.
               Salt Lake City, 3:00 p.m., St. Mark's
               Cathedral.
               Salt Lake City, 7:30 p.m., St. Paul's Church.
July 14-16...San Francisco, Convention
July 18.........San Francisco, 10:30 a.m., Trinity Church,
               Rev. A. W. Mann..
July 18.........Oakland, 10:30 a.m., St. Paul's Church,
               Dr. Gallaudet.
               San Francisco, 3:00 p.m. & 7:30 p.m.,
               Trinity Church.
July 19-23...San Francisco, at places to be duly announced.
July 25.........Fresno City, 7:30 p.m., St. James' Church.
July 30.........Santa Fe, 7:30 p.m., St. John's Church.

Some interesting comments on this journey were made
by T.Gallaudet in his Sketch, viz.--"We rested at Salt Lake
City for several days. Bishop Tuttle was absent but Mrs.
Tuttle was very hospitable. At Ogden we joined the special
excursion train conveying the great company of teachers
of deaf-mutes to the national convention at the California
Institution at Berkeley. We had a grand time crossing the
Rocky Mountains. At Sacramento City Mr. Wilkinson,
the Superintendent of the California Institution, met us
and gave us a hospitable breakfast with a warm welcome.
In due time we pressed on and were comfortably settled in
the Institution as guests of the great State of California....
The Reverend Mr. Mann and I held services in several of
the churches of Oakland and St. Francisco (sic).... On
Tuesday, July 27th, Mr. and Mrs. Mann and I reached Los
Angeles. Mr. and Mrs. Lee kindly entertained me. We met

Mr. Thomas Widd* and family, Mr. McGill and other deaf-mutes. We conducted services in St. Paul's Church. After a long railroad trip through southern California and New Mexico, we reached Santa Fe. On Sunday, August 1st, we conducted services in the Church of the Holy Faith, the Rev. Mr. Meany, Rector. and visited the School for the Deaf under Mr. Larson." (The visit to Santa Fe has already been reported in chapter 5.)

After the leave-taking of the Rev. and Mrs. Mann in Cleveland T.Gallaudet stopped at Buffalo on the way home and on Sunday, August 8, he held services in St. John's and St. Paul's Churches. On Monday evening, August 9, he had a combined service in the Sunday School room of St. Luke's Church, Rochester. From there he took a night train and reached home safely on Tuesday forenoon, August 10.

From this it would appear that the two missionaries would need a very long period of rest and recreation, to use a modern expression. But T.Gallaudet reported that soon after returning to New York City he went to Augusta, Ga., to officiate at the marriage of a deaf couple there. Then in October he attended a General Convention of the Church—the 35th—in Chicago; this was followed by the 3rd convention of the Conference of Church Workers Among the Deaf—now the Episcopal Conference of the Deaf. Of the latter the Rev Mr. Mann was the presiding officer.

---

* Mr. Thomas Widd for over a quarter of a century zealously and energetically prosecuted mission work among the deaf of Southern California as a licensed layreader. Before coming to California he was a pioneer educator of the deaf of Lower Canada, and for several years principal of the Mackay School for the Deaf at Montreal. He died on December 5, 1906, at the age of 67.

CHAPTER 8

Dr. Gallaudet's Trips Abroad

B y his many trips to Europe the Rev. Dr. Thomas Gallaudet made the countries he visited a part of his mission field; he became known and respected there, not only by clergy and educators of the deaf but by the many deaf people he encountered. The Sketch tells of eight trips abroad, but this autobiography came to an end in 1897 so other trips probably were not recorded there. His brother, Dr. Edward Miner Gallaudet, the founder and first president of Gallaudet University, stated that he made ten voyages to Europe. However, a careful perusal of old copies of the *Deaf-Mutes' Journal*—hereafter referred to as the Journal—printed between the years 1893 and 1901 may disclose even more than ten. While these were in part excursions for rest and recreation, there was always something for him to do on behalf of the deaf, particularly in England.

The first voyage was in 1880. In company with his wife Elizabeth and her companion Miss Gertrude C. Walter he took passage on the *Brittanic* in August of that year to attend, as a delegate of the New York school, the International Convention of Teachers of the Deaf and Dumb—as it was then called—to be held in Milan, Italy, in September. An account of the voyage, the trip from Queenstown in South Ireland, where they landed on August 23d, to Milan, the convention and places visited afterwards is given in one of T.Gallaudet's letters that was printed in the Journal (October 14) and is reproduced here.

The following letter from Rev. Thomas Gallaudet, D.D., to the parishioners of St. Ann's Church, was read by the Associate Rector, Rev. Mr. Kranz, Sunday, October 3d, being the Twenty-eighth Anniversary of the Parish:

Milan, Sept. 12, 1880.
"My Dear Friends and Parishioners:

"I send you greetings from this old city where St. Ambrose did such a great work about 1,500 years ago. Its central point is its magnificent Cathedral, second in size to St. Peter's in Rome. Besides this, there are eighty churches of the Roman Catholic Communion. Thus far, I have traveled rather rapidly through Cork, Dublin, Holyhead, London, Dover, Calais, Brussells, Basle, Luzerne, Pass St. Gotthard and the Italian Lakes, in order to be present at the opening of the International Convention of the Teachers of Deaf-Mutes in Milan on Monday, September 6th. Your prayers have been graciously answered, and our little party has thus far been wonderfully blessed.

"On the Twelfth Sunday after Trinity, August 14th, Rev. Dr. Forrrest, of Washington, D. C., and I conducted services on board the *Brittanic.* I spoke from the Gospel for the day (Mark 7:32,concerning a deaf man who was healed by Jesus), and so interested the passengers in our work among deaf-mute, that a large meeting was held the following Tuesday in the dining saloon, at which I was requested to go into detail, and explain the sign-language, and the manner of educating deaf-mutes. I think much good was done.

"On Sunday, August 22d, we had another good service on the ship.

"On Monday forenoon, the 23d, having left our noble ship at Queenstown, we attended prayers at St. Finn Barre's Cathedral in Cork and returned thanks. In Dublin we visited three institutions for deaf-mutes—one Church of England in Claremont, the other two (one for boys and one for girls) Roman Catholic in Carba—suburbs of the city. We were very kindly received, and much interested. All along my deaf-mute traveling companions and myself using our signs and finger alphabet attracted attention, and led to the giving of information. In Brussels, on Sunday morning, August 29th, I attended the English Church of the Resurrection. The Chaplain, Rev. Mr. Jenkins, invited me to join him in the service, which was musical and hearty, and to preach. The Holy Communion was celebrated. I made a short address on the Collect for the Fourteenth Sunday after Trinity and under Charity showed what had been done for deaf-mutes. The Chaplain said that the large congregation, who were very attentive, had received some new ideas. I visited the Institution for deaf-mutes at Brussels.

"As we came over the Alps we had silent sermons in rocks and rugged peaks, in waterfalls and valleys of Our Father's power and protecting care.

"Last Sunday and today I have attended services at the English church in an hall, tastefully arrayed with an altar, chancel, reading desk and pulpit at No. 11 Via Morigi. The Holy Communion is celebrated every Sunday. The seats are free and offerings are received for the support of the work. A society in England is planting English churches in all the principal cities of the continent. It is a blessed work.

"During the past week I have attended most of the sessions of the Convention, and visited the Institution for Deaf-Mutes in this city. There were delegates in large numbers from Italy and France, and in smaller numbers from Switzerland, Germany, Sweden, Norway, Great Britain, United States and Canada. Ladies as well as gentlemen, Sisters of Charity, members of the Brotherhood of St. Gabriel (these were from France), ecclesiastics and laymen, and differing in nationality and religious belief. All drawn together very closely by their love for those whom our Heavenly Father has seen fit to deprive of hearing and speech. It was really a picturesque and striking company composed of about 200 person. There were eight from America, including Dr. E. M. Gallaudet and Prof. Dennison of Washington, D.C., Dr. Stoddard, Dr. Peet, Miss Walter, Mrs. Gallaudet and myself of New York, and the Abbé Belanger of Montreal, and the same number from Great Britain. The majority of the Convention were in favor of using only articulation and lip-reading in the education of the deaf. There were a goodly number, however, including the Americans, who stood by the 'combined method, using both the sign-language, which has come down to us from the great philosophical teachers, De l'Epée, Sicard and Clerc, and the elder Gallaudet and Peet, and also articulation and lipreading for those who can be really benefitted thereby. I was very thankful to have the privilege of attending this Convention, and very grateful to all my friends who put it in my power to be there, and also to make a trip through part of Europe.

"On the second day of the Convention I made a short address, interpreted by Prof. Vaisse of Paris, showing the necessity of the sign-language in the full moral and spiritual, as well as intellectual, development of deaf-mutes, closing with our rendering of the Lord's Prayer in signs. Yesterday, the last day, I made one of the closing short speeches of thanks and good-will to our Italian hosts, and of brotherly feeling to all, though differing in views, yet acting according to the light of knowledge they had received. I have gained much good from the Convention, and I trust have done some good to others. The United States are doing more for the full education of the largest number of deaf-mutes than any European nation, and our pastoral care over adult deaf-mutes is more extensive and effective. St. Ann's pioneered this latter work and gave birth to the Church Mission to Deaf-Mutes.

"I often think of you all, and pray God's blessing to rest upon the whole parish, clergy and people, and also on all the work, the Sunday and week-day services, the Sunday School, the choir and the music and the Guild with its various departments. Asking your love and your prayers, I am

"Yours affectionately and faithfully,

"Thomas Gallaudet."

After the Convention adjourned the little party visited several famous cities in Italy, Switzerland, Austria and Germany. From Paris they returned to England, where they also visited cities of note. As they went about they had opportunity to visit several schools for the deaf. T.Gallaudet was especially interested in St. Saviour's Church in London, which was recognized as a spiritual and social center for the deaf of that city. They took the *Brittanic* again at Liverpool and after a stormy passage reached home on Christmas Day—"thankful to our Heavenly Father for all his mercies."

A person who is not familiar with methods of teaching the deaf and the mode of communication employed will discover that advocates of one system or the other are very partisan with respect to this. In his letter to the Journal T.Gallaudet pointed out that most of the European delegates to the Milan Convention favored the oral method of teaching, which began in Germany and favors only articulation* and lip-reading in the education of the deaf. However, "there were a goodly number, including the Americans, who stood by the 'combined method,' using both the sign-language.... and also articulation and lip-reading for those who can be really benefitted thereby."

Among the eight American delegates was Dr. Edward M. Gallaudet, president of Gallaudet College (now University) and brother of T.Gallaudet. In a paper entitled "The Influence of Dr. Thomas Gallaudet on Deaf-Mute Education in America"** President Gallaudet expressed his strong support for the manual/combined method of education and he pointed out that his brother, T.Gallaudet, had similar views. Excerpts from this paper are reprinted below.

In the early days of deaf-mute education two methods, quite different in their character, were made use of.

The basis of one was oral speech; that of the other the language of gesture and dactylology (known today as American Sign Language—ASL).

Under the first, the attempt was made to teach all deaf children to speak, and to understand the vocal utterances of others by observing the movement of the lips.

Those who taught by this method endeavored to give their pupils an education equivalent to that afforded in elementary schools.

Many of the promoters of the oral method undertook to keep their pupils from the language of signs and finger spelling, and few made any use in class-room of these most natural means of communication with the deaf.

---

* Terms used today are Speech and Speech-reading.

** This paper was made an addition to T.Gallaudet's Sketch after his death in 1902. A copy is in the repository of the Gallaudet University Archives.

Under the second method no attempt was made to teach speech or lipreading. The natural language of the deaf, that of gestures, was cultivated and made much of as a means of reaching the intelligence and influencing the conduct of the children long before any adequate channel of communication could be established by means of speech.

Finger spelling was resorted to as an exact and convenient means of familiarizing the deaf child with words and their combinations in verbal language.

Upon this basis quite full and satisfactory elementary education was built up as was attained under the oral method.

For fully a century the two methods just described were pursued with no attempt at combination, the former being often called the German method and the latter the French because of their having been invented and practiced in Germany and France respectively.

During the first half-century of deaf-mute education in this country, the method pursued was the Manual, derived from the great school in Paris in 1816. And it may be said, in passing, that under this method the deaf children of the United States were given a school training which transformed them from helpless, almost hopeless beings into happy, self-reliant, self-supporting members of society.

In 1867 two schools for the deaf, modeled after those of Germany, were established in this country. This new departure attracted the attention of the managers of the older schools, and one or two prominent instructors were sent to Europe to examine schools for the deaf there, with a view of ascertaining whether any change in the method theretofore practised in America was desirable. The reports of these investigators and the results shown in the two schools just alluded to, led the authorities of other schools in the country to recommend that all deaf children should have an opportunity to learn to speak. They were not convinced, however, that it would be for the interests of these children to adopt the German or Oral Method to the exclusion of the other. And so it came about that a combination was soon effected in the larger schools of the country, which has become general and which is now recognized in educational circles throughout the world as the Combined System.

His varied and extended intercourse with the deaf has afforded him unusual opportunity to judge the results of the different methods, for, in addition to the many naturally coming from manual schools, large numbers of those whose education has been conducted in purely oral schools, have connected themselves with the organizations in which he has been prominent; and this in spite of the injunctions of their teachers against the use of the language of signs and against the association of the deaf together.

There were two prominent reasons why Dr. Gallaudet opposed the exclusive use of the Oral Method in the education of the deaf.

First, because his intercourse with those taught in this way satisfied him that great numbers did not succeed in acquiring a facility in speech that was at all commensurate with the amount of time and labor expended theron.

His observations had made it clear that many deaf children of average mental ability, and some with more than this, were not able to become successful speakers and lip-readers.

The best speech these could acquire was so imperfect, and often so disagreeable to those who heard it, and consequently so hard to understand as to cause those who used it to be shunned by others.

This treatment wounded and discouraged these unsuccessful deaf speakers to such an extent that in many cases they gave up trying to speak and resorted to writing.

Dr. Gallaudet's opinion was that in all such cases it would have been better if the time given to speech teaching had been devoted, under the Manual Method, to useful matters where success was possible.

His second reason for opposing the exclusive use of the Oral Method was because under it the language of signs is discredited and little used.

And here should be considered the prolonged and intimate intercourse with mother and wife which has been alluded to.

Dr. Gallaudet learned to talk with his fingers before he could use his tongue to express his thoughts and wishes.

In the home circle, as he grew up, the mimic language was co-existent with the vocal, and naturally the language of the mother was resorted to as often as the other.

These conditions continued in his own family after his marriage, and with this experience he was able in the years of his maturity to judge intelligently to what extent the use of the language of signs added to the happiness of the deaf, or detracted from it....

In his advocacy of the use of the sign language, Dr. Gallaudet always took pains to disclaim all purpose in undervaluing the effort to teach speech and lip-reading where this could be done successfully.

In forming an estimate of the influence of Dr. Gallaudet on deaf-mute education in this country, many matters besides his opinions as to methods must be considered.

His position as a member of the boards of directors of several schools in New York State and elsewhere, gave him opportunities to advocate, as he always did, for deaf children, the fullest, broadest training, morally, mentally, and physically, which they were capable of receiving. He was an interested and earnest supporter of the College for the Deaf at Washington, always advising any young deaf-mutes of ability with whom he came in contact, to become students therein if possible.

While he favored the formation of societies of the deaf, for social intercourse and literary culture, he advised them not to confine themselves to associations with each other, but to come into all possible relations with hearing people.

There is every reason to believe that Dr. Gallaudet's opinions and his advice had great weight with the majority of teachers of the deaf in this country, but behind and above all that he thought and said, his greatest power lay in what he was....

* * *

Dr. Gallaudet's second trip overseas was made in 1883 on July 14th, again on the *Brittanic* of the White Star Line. Details of this trip are given in his Sketch; also the 11th annual report to the Church Mission to Deaf-Mutes, 1884. Excerpts from the report follow.

The latter part of July I attended the annual convention of the National Society of Adult Deaf-Mutes in Great Britain & Ireland, held in a lecture room of St. Saviour's Church for Deaf-Mutes, Oxford Street, London. I was also present at several services in that church. The English signs, however, differ so radically from ours that I was obliged to make my address though an interpreter....

I was in Brussels from Saturday evening, August 11th, to Tuesday morning, the 21st. On the 12th and 19th I officiated (at) the English Church of the Resurrection   The International Convention of Teachers of the Deaf began its service on Monday, the 18th, and adjourned on Saturday afternoon, the 19th. It was held in the Palais des Academies at the invitation of the government. King Leopold II was present at one of the sessions. I represented the Church Mission to Deaf-Mutes and the New York Institution (school) for the Deaf-Mutes in this convention. Various practical questions were discussed, and representative men and women became better acquainted. We visited the schools for deaf-mutes in Brussels, Ghent and Antwerp. There were several members at the convention from the United States....

On my second Sunday afternoon in Brussels I was present at the service of about 25 deaf-mute men and women held in a Lutheran Church. As their signs, in common with ours, are taken from the French, I was able to officiate (for) them, and I was told afterwards that they clearly understood me.

After brief visits to Paris and Havre I returned to England and visited several of the cathedrals.

I left Liverpool on the *Brittanic* on the 6th of September and reached home on Sunday morning, the 16th, just in time for the service at St. Ann's Church. During my nine weeks of absence I had been providentially guided and blessed.

* * *

On June 3, 1888, being the 66th anniversary of his birthday, T.Gallaudet embarked on his third trip to Europe aboard the Cunard Royal Mail Steamship *Aurania* as the guest of "my good friend Mr. Frederic Goodridge." The Rev. Dr. Langford, Secretary of the Board of Missions, was a fellow passenger, and with him T.Gallaudet attended a meeting of the Society for the Propagation of the Gospel to Foreign Parts. Later, after a trip through Scotland, he attended a service held in connection with the Lambeth Conference of Bishops in Canterbury Cathedral and Westminster Abbey. At a garden party following this he met the Archbishop of Canterbury, to whom he introduced himself and made a brief reference to his work with the deaf. Before returning home T.Gallaudet and Mr. Goodridge enjoyed an extended journey through France, Switzerland, the Rhineland and Holland. He reached home on September 18.

An account of T.Gallaudet's fourth trip to Europe, in 1889, is contained in a letter addressed to Mr. E. A. Hodgson, editor of the Journal and a vestryman of St. Ann's Church. The letter, written aboard the Steamship *Aurania*, on September 11, was printed in the Journal. It ran to almost two columns of 8 point type.

On this trip T.Gallaudet accompanied a group of 25 deaf men, representatives of various organizations in the United States who were on their way to an International Congress of the Deaf held in Paris. Before going to France the group was received by the Royal Association in the Aid of the Deaf and Dumb at a public meeting in London on July 8th, according to a news item in the *Deaf and Dumb Times* (July,1889). Included in this group were three deaf missionaries of the Episcopal Church, namely, the Rev. Messrs. Jacob Koehler, Job Turner and James H. Cloud. What impressed T.Gallaudet about the Congress, held July 10-18, was, as he said, "the tribute of love and esteem to the Abbé de l'Epée, in its recognition of (Abbé Roch-Ambroise-Curran) Sicard, (T.H.) Gallaudet, (Laurent) Clerc and (Harvey Prindle) Peet, as succeeding benefactors of deaf-mutes, and its suggestion of a common sign-language for all nations."

After visiting briefly in London, T.Gallaudet went to Cork, Ireland, where he was met by Mr. Francis Maginn, a deaf lay missionary, with whom he became acquainted when Mr. Maginn was a student at Gallaudet University in Washington, D. C. An account of his ministry was printed in the *British Deaf-Mutes and Deaf Chronicle* of January, 1893. Below are excerpts.

To trace the growth of the Society, under whose auspices Mr. Maginn pursues his work, we must go back to the year 1873, when the late Miss Tredennick, who has for many years previously been actively interesting herself in the adult deaf and dumb, took steps to form a society called "The Deaf and Dumb Christian Association"

The work grew and found many warm supporters, chiefly, we feel bound to say, owing to the disinterestedness, zeal, unwearied, self-denying labours of Miss Tredennick and her sister, Mrs. Kingstone, who made the cause of the deaf and dumb of Ireland their own, and worked on in faith and hope when many would have relinquished the task in despair. In

1881, Mr. R. S, Lyons went to the National Deaf-Mute College, Washington, to qualify himself with a view to his being appointed Missionary.   In 1884 Mr. Maginn went out to Washington, being sent there by his friends, who were desirous that he should take a College degree if possible.   In April, 1885, Mr. Lyons became dangerously ill, and was ordered home and Mr. Maginn accompanied him, and took care of him on the voyage.   Mr. Lyons died shortly after his arrival, and Mr. Maginn was thus left to return to America alone.   Before doing so, he undertook a Mission tour in the North of Ireland, in the course of which he visited Belfast, and made the acquaintance of his future charge.

In this year the society was re-organized under the title of "Missions to the Adult Deaf and Dumb of Ireland," the Lord Bishop of Cork kindly consenting to be President.

In 1887, on the death of his father, the Rev. C. A. Maginn, who for many years was Rector and Rural Dean of Castletown-roche, Co. Cork, Mr. Maginn was compelled to abandon the hope of remaining at Washington, until he had completed his course and taken his degree.   He returned home in June, and has since been continuously engaged in Missionary work in Ireland.   At first he was stationed at Cork where he has commenced a Sunday service, in the year 1883, assisted by Mrs. Kingstone and Miss Austin.   This service is still continued, being conducted by Mr. F. S. Bence, who was appointed Catechist in 1890, when it was found impossible for Mr. Maginn to reside six months in Cork and six in Belfast, as had been at first arranged....

With respect to his visit to Ireland and Mr. Maginn T.Gallaudet wrote in his letter to Editor Hodgson—

Under the guidance of his kind and devoted friend, I enjoyed for upwards of a month the generous hospitality of the friends of deaf-mutes in Ireland, and made many very pleasant acquaintances among the bishops and other clergy and the residents of several of the chief cities of the beautiful island.

I attended gatherings of deaf-mutes and also meetings of hearing people specially appointed for me to give information in relation to missions to adult deaf-mutes; made addresses and preached sermons in Cork, Dublin, Kingstown, Monkstown and Belfast.   On Sunday afternoon, July 28th, I preached to a large congregation in the Cathedral of Cork....

Arriving in Belfast Wednesday night, August 7th, we were welcomed by Miss Tredennick to the Central Hall and Office of the Irish Society, at No. 7 Fisherwick Place. In addition to accommodations for the lady-in-charge and the missionary, this building contains a chapel, a reading-room and recreation rooms. God has wonderfully blessed this venture of faith and its purifying, elevating influences have greatly promoted the temporal as well as spiritual interests of the deaf-mutes of this thrifty city of 250,000 inhabitants. I remained there three Sundays, and in five churches tried to give the congregations some information concerning the sign-language, the education of deaf-mutes and the progress of Church work among them, with the chief idea of strengthening the Irish Society. Miss Tredennick and Mr. Maginn were pleased to say that I had been providentially sent to encourage them at the right time....

On Sunday afternoon, (August 18), we had a celebration of the Holy Communion in All Saints' Church, and in the evening I preached to a deaf-mute congregation at the Bethel. On several occasions, during my delightful sojourn in Belfast, I addressed my deaf-mute friends in the chapel of the Central Hall. By spelling some words with the double-handed alphabet and using natural signs, I succeeded in making myself quite generally understood. I considered it a great privilege to have become so well acquainted with Miss Tredennick, who for twenty years has proved herself to be a loving and faithful friend to the deaf-mutes of Ireland....(T.Gallaudet reported in his Sketch that in the year 1891 Miss Wilhelmina Tredennick was "taken to her rest.")

T.Gallaudet was in Ireland from July 24 to August 26. Then he went to Scotland, where he met and enjoyed the hospitality of deaf missionaries, visited schools for the deaf and other institutions, as well as enjoying some sightseeing at famous places such as the cottage where the poet Robert Burns was born and "the wonderful bridge across the Firth of Forth." He remained in Scotland until September 7, then took passage on the *Aurania* to make the return voyage home. He arrived home September 16. He had been gone since June 28.

An account of T.Gallaudet's fifth trip to England in 1891—from July 18 to October 5—appeared in the *New York Times,* Oct. 6 issue. Excerpts are reprinted here.

Dr. Gallaudet on this trip spoke in sixteen different churches and also in various meeting halls in England, Scotland and Ireland. Between four and five thousand persons were addressed. He took occasion to impress the value of the sign language to express the ideas, to urge the utility of boarding schools in place of more day schools for the afflicted; to advocate training in industries in these schools after study hours; and to ask for Government aid in these efforts to improve the condition of the deaf.

At present in England no Government aid is extended to the teaching of the deaf and dumb. At the last session of Parliament a bill was passed providing such aid in Scotland, and at the next session it is expected that a similar enactment will be made for England and Ireland.

Much interest was manifested in Dr. Gallaudet's account of the work done by the Protestant Episcopal Church in America in behalf of deaf-mutes. There are now in this country ten Episcopalian clergymen who can minister to the deaf and dumb, and four of these are themselves deaf-mutes. In this country about 40,000 persons are totally deaf, and there are about one half as many in the United Kingdom.

The meeting of the British Deaf and Dumb Association was held in Glasgow during the first week in August. Dr. Gallaudet and his brother, Dr. E. M. Gallaudet, of the National Deaf-Mutes College at Washington, attended the sessions. Their presence was due to Mr. Francis Maginn, an Irish deaf-mute missionary, who was for two and one-half years a pupil (sic) at the National Deaf-Mute College in Washington, where he acquired the American methods. He had the managers of the British associations write, inviting the Messrs. Gallaudet.

The Rev. Dr. Gallaudet read two papers before the Association—one on the missions to the adult deaf and dumb and the other on the homes for aged and infirm deaf-mutes. Prof. Gallaudet of Washington read an elaborate paper on the value of the combined method of teaching. The discussions of the association were in the sign language, and the papers were interpreted in that language....

Not mentioned in the Times article was that T.Gallaudet was accompanied on this trip by a deaf priest, the Rev. Jacob M. Koehler, missioner to the deaf in Central

Pennsylvania.   Another deaf man, the Rev. James H. Cloud, ordained a deacon in 1889, held services for the Rev. Mr. Koehler while he was absent.

*   *   *

Seven other trips overseas were taken by T.Gallaudet, the last one being in 1901, which was one year before his death on August 27, 1902.   On three of these trips he was accompanied by the Rev. A. W. Mann, a deaf priest who planned the trip to California in 1886 with T.Gallaudet. In 1898 four Americans attended the 4th Congress of the British Deaf & Dumb Association that was held in the lecture hall of St. Saviour's Church for the Deaf & Dumb in London.

Accounts of these trips are found in the Sketch and/or the Journal; also in annual reports of T.Gallaudet to the Church Mission to Deaf-Mutes, and reports of the New York School for the Deaf.

CHAPTER 9

Last Years Of Ministry

I n chapter four it was reported that in 1892, at the age of 70, T.Gallaudet retired as rector of St. Ann's Church for the Deaf. But his retirement years were far from sedentary. For one thing, as reported in the previous chapter, he made some five trips abroad before his death in 1902. These trips overseas involved him in much activity, particularly in England and Ireland.

AT CHICAGO. In 1893 T.Gallaudet attended the World Congress of the Deaf in Chicago and, concurrently, the 8th convention of the Conference of Church Workers Among the Deaf (now the Episcopal Conference of the Deaf), held at All Angels' Church for the Deaf, which had been dedicated for use by the deaf the year before. Four deaf priests and several lay people were in attendance at both the Congress and the convention at All Angels'.

GOLDEN WEDDING ANNIVERSARY. In 1895 T.Gallaudet and his wife, Elizabeth Budd Gallaudet, celebrated their 50th wedding anniversary. In the July 18th issue of the *Deaf-Mutes' Journal* there was a 5-column write-up about this event. Later, in the *Gallaudet Alumni Bulletin* (Vol. 3, No. 9), the celebration was described in considerable detail by Mr. Lawrence Newman, class of 1948, as follows:

By the stir and bustle that preceded the celebration of the Golden Wedding Anniversary of the Rev. Dr. and Mrs. Thomas Gallaudet one would think that preparations were being made for the inauguration of the President of the United States. Plans were plotted a year before the celebration. The Gallaudet Half-Century Association was organized by the deaf of New York in 1894 (under the leadership of Mr. William G. Fitzgerald) and included executive, finance, and ladies' auxiliary committees.

A fund was established by the Association and the collections represented, according to the words printed in the souvenir program, "the contributions of 3,925 individuals, the uniform sum of 10 cents having been fixed as the amount of each donation in order to render the fund a truly representative testimonial of the deaf of New York City and vicinity without regard to social position or worldly possessions."

The main ceremonies took place in the New York school chapel. The audience stood and saluted as the procession with the honored guests at the head passed through the main aisle on the way to the head of the chapel.

Principal Currier of the school delivered the address of welcome. Then the president of the Half-Century Association, Mr. William G. Fitzgerald eulogized the honored couple. The Gallaudets received $133 in gold in a neat morocoo case from the deaf of Pennsylvania, a large bouquet of flowers from the deaf of Boston and after a testimonial address by the Half-Century Association, Edith Pedlowe, a five-year-old pupil, presented the New York testimonial—a bag of gold coin in the amount of $300. At this presentation Dr. Gallaudet expressed his gratitude and related tales of family incidents throughout the 50 years. When he ceased, letters and telegrams of congratulations were read by Dr. Thomas Fox.

After renditions of specially written poems, Dr. Edward M. Gallaudet, the President of Gallaudet College, talked briefly in speech and signs about his brother, the Rev. Gallaudet, and sister-in-law.

Addresses were made by Rev. Mr. Chamberlain, Rev. Job Turner of Virginia, and Rev. Dr. DeCosta, pastor of the Church of St. John the Evangelist, and as a finale to the exercises, Mr. William G. Jones signed "Auld Lang Syne."

After the literary exercises the guests dined at the school and later on in the evening danced to the tunes of an orchestra that was hired for the occasion.

A NEW ST. ANN'S. Already reported—in Chapter 4—are the events attendant upon the sale of old St. Ann's Church at West 18th Street and Fifth Avenue for the sum of $200,000, the proposed merger with St. Matthew's Church

---

A PLEASANT SURPRISE

As usual T.Gallaudet was in Washington, D.C., for the Presentation Day ceremonies (commencement) of Gallaudet College on May 2, 1900. On the program of this ceremony he saw his name printed as the one who would give the benediction. So he was unprepared for an event that had not been announced. With the last-minute approval of the Board of Trustees, his youngest brother, Edward, who was president of the institution, conferred upon him the honorary degree of Doctor of Humane Letters "in recognition of his long successful labors in the moral elevation of the educated deaf.

---

at West 84th Street, then the decision to relocate a new St. Ann's Church at 148th Street, and its consecration on December 26, 1898. Of the consecration, T.Gallaudet said in his Sketch, "It was a momentous occasion." And with that his autobiography comes to an end.

FIRE AT THE HOME. It was a great shock to T.Gallaudet to receive word, in 1900, that the Home for Aged and Infirm Deaf-Mutes at Poughkeepsie, N.Y., was completely destroyed by a fire of undetermined origin the evening of

Sunday, February 18th. According to the Journal twenty inmates were saved from the building by the heroism of the nurses and Isaac Gardiner, the Home gardener. And further: "some of the residents were blind as well as deaf, and the early discovery of the fire alone prevented a frightful scene. The building stood on a hill on the bank of the Hudson, and the cold wind fanned the flames into instant conflagration. The Home was established in 1885 through the earnest and steadfast efforts of the Rev. Dr. Thomas Gallaudet.—Feb. 22 issue. Later, in 1903 the same paper could report in a featured story in its January 1 issue that a new Gallaudet Home for the Aged and infirm Deaf—a fine, fireproof building midway between New Hamburgh and Poughkeepsie in New York—had arisen, figuratively speaking, from the ashes of the first one. The formal dedication and opening of the new Home was held on June 3, the birthday anniversary of the Rev. Dr. Thomas Gallaudet, by whom it was founded and watched over until his death in 1902.

A GOLDEN JUBILEE. On Saturday, June 28th, 1900, at St. Matthew's Church on 84th Street in New York City, began the celebration of the 50 years of ministry—as an ordained priest—of the Rev. Thomas Gallaudet, D.D., L.H.D.

According to the Journal, in its July 4 issue, there was a very large gathering of Church dignitaries, including the Rt. Rev. Henry C. Potter, Bishop of New York, besides a large congregation of friends.

"In the evening at General Theological Seminary, a quintuplet of venerable priests were each presented with a loving cup by Bishop Potter at memorial services at which the full vested choir of Trinity Church participated. Dr. Gallaudet also received a purse of money from the people of St. Matthew's (and St. Ann's Church for the Deaf).

"On Sunday, the 30th (of June), St. Ann's Church was filled to overflowing with deaf friends of Dr. Gallaudet, to further honor him. Vested and in procession was Dr. Gallaudet himself and the Rev. Dr. Charles M. Niles, rector of St. Paul's Church, Ossining, N.Y., Rev. Dr. John Chamberlain, (and the four deaf priests), the Rev. Messrs.

Austin W. Mann, J. M. Koehler, Job Turner and C. O. Dantzer; also Layreader Chester Q. Mann. Testimonial addresses were given by each of the clergy present, and letters of regret were read from those who could not come and participate in the celebration. At Dr. Gallaudet's request, Mr. E. A. Hodgson spoke briefly.

"One of the out-of-town visitors at St. Ann's that day was Dr. Edward Miner Gallaudet, president of Gallaudet College in Washington, the youngest brother of the Rev. Dr. Gallaudet (by 15 years). Asked to speak to the assemblage, Dr. E. M. Gallaudet responded by saying with regard to his brother, 'his whole life was a series of good and gentle deeds. He never was known to speak in anger.' To illustrate this attribute of Rev. Dr. Gallaudet's character he told how, when Thomas Gallaudet was marching in the procession of graduates at Trinity College, clad in cap and gown, that he, then a little boy of five years, had run up to him and taken hold of his hand. Instead of a rebuke for such a liberty on that all-important occasion, Dr. Gallaudet held to the little hand and together they walked along.

"The chairman of the committee on arrangements presented the Rev. Dr. Gallaudet, as from his deaf friends, one hundred dollars in gold. The celebration of the golden jubilee was concluded with a benediction, pronounced by the Rev. Dr. Thomas Gallaudet."

DEATH COMES TO T. GALLAUDET. The death and funeral of T. Gallaudet have already been set down in the Introduction of this work. It was the passing of a great and good man. In another chapter will be set down testimonials to his greatness and extraordinary accomplishments.

In an essay entitled "A Brief History of St. Ann's Church for the Deaf and its Founder, the Rev. Dr. Thomas Gallaudet" by the Rev. Eric Whiting—mentioned in chapter 3—the following is said:

> The January 2nd, 1902, issue of the *Deaf-Mutes' Journal* reported that the Reverend Dr. Gallaudet was very sick. At one stage of his illness he was kept alive only with oxygen.

His condition was described as muscular weakness of the heart.

Prior to his illness, Dr. Gallaudet had appealed to the congregation to organize a social evening. Prompt to obey, such an evening was hold on Tuesday, January 4th.

A later edition of the *Deaf-Mutes' Journal* reports that Dr. Gallaudet began to improve slowly, and his doctors have confidence that the Spring will find him once more among his deaf-mute friends. Of course, he may be able to go about long before the Spring, but at his advanced age, 80, it is better to make haste slowly, so that the recovery will be complete.

By March the DMJ was able to report that the Rev. Dr. Gallaudet was out for a short walk a week ago. Again—this week—he is strong enough to take an occasional carriage ride.

Later in March the DMJ again reports, "If the weather is pleasant the Rev. Dr. Gallaudet will be present at the Easter services in St. Ann's Church for Deaf-Mutes. It will be the first time he has been at the church since he was taken ill a little before Christmas." However, by the time Easter arrived Dr. Gallaudet was still not strong enough to be with his beloved people.

An impressive birthday party was scheduled for Dr. Gallaudet's 80th birthday, Tuesday, June 3rd, 1902. The affair was held in the Guild Rooms of St. Ann's, and the advertisements for the party included the notice that "If weather conditions are favorable, Rev. Dr. Gallaudet will be present."

Much to the delight of all the members and friends of St. Ann's, Dr. Gallaudet did attend the lavish party at which he was the guest of honor.

On Sunday, June 6th, it was expected that Dr. Gallaudet would officiate at the services at St. Ann's. In fact, a choir made up of five young ladies was to render hymns in concert, in the language of signs. The large congregation in attendance at St. Ann's, hoping to hear Dr. Gallaudet, was disappointed. He was not able to attend because he caught cold while at his birthday party, and his doctors advised him to remain at home.

By mid-August Dr. Gallaudet's cold having not improved, he made a brief visit to the New Jersey coast, hoping for some relief. Upon his return to New York he suffered a relapse.

The Reverend Dr. Thomas Gallaudet left this life at nine o'clock on the morning of August 27th, 1902. His untiring work with the deaf people throughout the world has earned him the unofficial title of "Apostle to the Deaf."

Mrs. Gallaudet was in her 79th year when she died in 1903. This was just a few months after her husband's death.

CHAPTER 10

The Good Old Days

This chapter is a reprint from the January 1958 issue of St. Ann's Bulletin, *published by St. Ann's Church for the Deaf. The author, Alex L. Pach, was a deaf photographer of note, who had a photographic establishment, first at Easton, Pa., then later at 111 Broadway, New York City.*

I t was in 1897 that most all the deaf of New York toiled up the hill from the 145th Street elevated station to 511 West 148th Street to see Dr. Gallaudet and other church dignitaries lay the cornerstone of what was the new St. Ann's, and, of course, this was before New Yorkers had subways. It was a big jump upward from 18th Street and Fifth Avenue, which had been the center of most of New York's activities so far as the deaf were concerned.

Besides the activities of St. Ann's Church, and its Guild of Silent Workers, the Manhattan Literary Association met there on Thursday evenings, and it was an open forum for the deaf of all denominations; and the only other organization for the deaf was the Catholic Literary and Benevolent Union. Fanwood graduates predominated, as there were only a few active workers in evidence from the other schools for the deaf. The 23rd Street (Public School) was then undreamed of.

On Sunday afternoons and Thursday evenings 18th Street was New York's most popular gathering place, and after the Sunday services a majority of those in attendance adjourned to the Fifth Avenue Hotel, then at 23rd Street, where they were met by many others in that section of the hotel which was know as the "Amen Corner" because on weekdays it was the headquarters of Republican Leader Tom Platt and his yes-men of the party.

The proprietors of the hotel, Messrs. Hitchcock and Darling, were both friends of Dr. Gallaudet, and they encouraged the deaf to make that section of the hotel their meeting place.

If a moving picture of a gathering of the deaf of that day were shown to an audience today there would be much merriment. Ladies with hoop–skirts, bustles, dirt–sweeping dresses and monstrous feather-bedecked hats. Most of the men wore what was known as Prince Albert coats, and quite a number came in silk hats—plug hats they were called—and cost us ten dollars each.

The hearing portion of Dr. Gallaudet's congregation met just before the services for the deaf were held, the former coming out as the latter entered. Among the hearing attendants were many of New York's so–called "Four Hundred." Dr. Gallaudet was much beloved by his hearing congregation as he was by his deaf flock, and by many people of other denominations who, having no services that they could call their own, made St. Ann's their church home. Proselyting was unknown in this church and no questions were asked unless one applied for membership. The fact that a person was deaf was the open sesame to a glad hand of fellowship, and this extended to

---

BITS OF HISTORY

The New York City Commercial Telephone Exchange opened during the fall of 1878 with a phone directory consisting of one single page with a listing of 252 names-of business establishments. You didn't need a telephone number; you just asked the male operator for your party by name. It was not until 1902 that the name "Rev. Thomas Gallaudet" appeared in the directory; this was the year of his death. His address was listed as 112 W. 78th St. Also listed was Bern Budd Gallaudet, M.D., his son, a physician, at 60 W. 50th St. Previosuly, in 1896, appeared the name of Peter Wallace Gallaudet, a brother of T.Gallaudet, listed as a "note broker" (a financier) whose address was 2 Wall St., cor. Broadway.

• • •

New York's subway, the Interborough, which ran from one end of Manhattan to the other and through a part of the Bronx, was opened in 1904. So T.Gallaudet never enjoyed the luxury of traveling through the city on its fast trains.

---

the hearing people who, though they did not know the deaf people except by sight, were most cordial in their exchange of greetings as they emerged from the church.

Two of the hearing members stand out clear in memory, perhaps the clearer because they were so active in the Dramatic Society that was made up of St. Ann's membership. There was a niece of Bishop Potter, popularly known as "Fifi" Potter, who afterward become the wife of President Stillman of the National City Bank, and who might have become a professional actress had she cared to. And there was Edward Fales Coward, endowed with the same histrionic talent as Miss Potter and also like Miss Potter a scion of a distinguished family, but who instead became a journalist and one of the leading drama critics of his day. He was on the New York World staff for many years and the present writer enjoyed his friendship.

The Gallaudet Club and the League of Elect Surds were outgrowths of gatherings at St. Ann's when their respective founders were unable to fill social requirements of the club type with what the Manhattan Literary Association offered, though in its day and in its time the M.L.A.'s lectures, debates etc., were well worth a trip by a Brooklynite, who, for instance, had to pay fares on two ferry boats and four lines of street cars, or if he came to New York by the Fulton Ferry, as most of them did, he used a Fifth Avenue Bus of that day which was horse drawn and carried him straight from the New York terminus of the ferry to Fifth Avenue and 18th Street. There was only a roundabout way of reaching the church from the Bronx and it wasn't even called the Bronx then, as people were from Morrisiana or Claremont or Mt. Hope or any of several other towns north of the Harlem River, which are now lumped categorically as the Bronx. The Union League of the Deaf, the National Fraternal Society, the Knights and Ladies of De l'Epée, the Ephpheta and other organizations were all of a later day.

If there were enough of us today to bring it about, and if our memories were retentive enough, we could electrify a deaf audience of today with a replica of a meeting of the Manhattan Literary Association I remember a debate by four of the leading men of that day on a topic that had to do with the relative "awfulness" (honest!) of fire on the one hand and water on the other. I had witnessed a similar debate on the same question while a school boy at Fanwood, but was not then familiar enough with the sign language to gather the fine points. Sometimes the debate had to do with the desirability of country life as contrasted with city life. Then we had splendid lectures, notably those given by Dr. Gallaudet, who was a type of man and type of cleric we rarely meet nowadays. He loved the people of the deaf world, and made no distinction between those who were members of his flock and those who were not.

He attended all our social affairs: Balls, Entertainments and Picnics; and he was able to call most everyone by name, and knew if an individual had recently met with misfortune. He read the *Deaf-Mutes' Journal* and knew all that was going on in the deaf world, not only in New York city and state but in Boston, Providence, Hartford and other New England points where he preached regularly. At the time of his death, in 1902, we of the Empire State Association were in session at Troy, and it cast gloom over our proceedings as he had been with us at our previous meetings as well as being a regular attendant at meetings of the National Association of the Deaf.

It is just forty years ago that St. Ann's moved to its present location—then very sparsely built—and it was thought that Dr. Gallaudet's selection of the site was in order to be near the Fanwood School, and now after four decades, ironically enough, the Fanwood School is moving further north.

A few steps from Old St. Ann's Church at 18th Street the Lexington School for the Deaf held its annual graduation exercises in Chickering Hall. These events attracted most of the prominent men of that day. Within a mile of Old St. Ann's nearly all of the activities of the deaf were consummated. The Catholic deaf, then as now, worshipped at St. Francis Xavier's, 16th Street; our Banquets were held at Clark's and at the Fleichsman Restuarant at Broadway and 10th Street. The Fanwood Quad Club, the predecessor of the League of Elect Surds, met at 17th Street and Third Avenue; so, with the Fifth Avenue Hotel rendezvous, all the doings of the New York of that day took place in the heart of the city. And, likewise, the Reverand Thomas Gallaudet, D.D., occupied a major place in the hearts of all those New Yorkers who knew him, and their name was legion.

•   •   •   •

Memories of A Brooklynite

A man who could remember when the bridges across the East River in New York had not been built and the subways had not yet been invented—was Mr. Archibald MacLaren, who was feted at the 50th anniversary dinner of the Brooklyn Protestant Guild of the Deaf, held January 17, 1942.

On January 7, 1892, the Rev. Dr. Thomas Gallaudet, Missionary to the Deaf, called the deaf of Brooklyn together to form a society of their own. Mr. MacLaren was one of the seven men who came to the first meeting to organize the Guild. In addition to business meetings, they had church services in St. Mark's Church and St. David's Church for the Deaf, which was started by the Rev. Dr. Colt, an assistant of Dr. Gallaudet.

Mr. MacLaren was born in Kingston, Ontario, on January 9, 1866. From earliest infancy he was deaf, as were a large number of other Canadian children. In 1870 a government school was established in the town of Belleville for their education, and Archibald MacLaren was sent to this institution. After completing the school course, he lived in Prescott, Ont., opposite Ogdensburg, N.Y., across the St. Lawrence River. He started his career in the industrial world by working in a malt–house. In December, 1888, he moved to New York City and found work for one year as a painter. Then he became an ironworker in a concern which manufactured wire and other metallic products; and in this line of industry he continued until he retired. In New York he met and married a deaf girl named Catherine Colligan. He also became a naturalized citizen of the United States.

In the "good old days," said Mr. MacLaren, when the Guild came into existence, and the deaf of Brooklyn wished to go to St. Ann's Church for the Deaf to attend social gatherings, it was necessary to go by ferry–boat and by horse–car. In the cold winters, this was an almost superhuman achievement: but, he added, the deaf of that day were used to such hardships.—*The Silent Missionary* (vol. 18, no. 10).

CHAPTER 11

Tributes/Testimonials

T here are so many testimonials to the greatness and goodness of the Rev. Dr. Thomas Gallaudet—in sermons, eulogies, editorials, memorials, and the like—that if all were brought together in printed form they would certainly comprise a volume of considerable size.

The first of these is excerpts from an editorial written up for the DMJ—printed the day after the death of T.Gallaudet—by Mr. Edwin A. Hodgson, editor and for many years a vestryman of St. Ann's Church.

> *"No more his kindly glances meet us gravely;*
> *His hand points backward to the path he trod;*
> *Dear one, we know you fought and struggled bravely,*
> *And died upon the battlefield of God."*

A friend of humankind has passed away. The best–loved and trusted friend of the deaf of this and past generations has gone to his reward. Rev. Dr. Thomas Gallaudet is at rest in Paradise, and thousands of deaf-mutes are plunged in deepest sorrow. He died yesterday, Wednesday, August the twenty-seventh, at nine o'clock in the morning. Since Sunday last he had been unconscious, caused by water on the brain, the result of the heart trouble which for a year or more had kept him in a state of feebleness. Although it was widely known that his life could not be prolonged, his death came as a shock to all. It was supposed that he would gradually wear away and that a fatal termination might occur within a few months; but none of those outside his immediate family knew of the near approach of death. The JOURNAL had already been printed, and the editor was on his way to the convention of the Empire State Association of the Deaf at Troy, when the sad news reached him. He returned at once, and this is a second edition of the JOURNAL of this week. . . .

Up to a year ago, Rev. Dr. Gallaudet was strong and vigorous as the ordinary man many years his junior. He was then in his eightieth year. The Holy Scripture tells us, "The days of our age are threescore and ten; and though men be so strong that they come to four score years, yet is their strength, then, but labor and sorrow; so soon it passeth away." And so it was with Rev. Dr. Gallaudet. His physical ailments began to manifest themselves in a decided way. He was taken sick; recovered, again was seized by sickness, and on Christmas Day of 1901 it was thought his time to say farewell to the world had arrived. However, he rallied, and although it seemed he might again get something of his one–time strength, many of his intimate friends could see the firm footsteps of decay were stealing on. But so great was his love for the deaf, that even in his sickbed he wrote and dictated and planned in their behalf. He was at once the most spiritual and the most human of men. He accepted every burden with patience, and gave God the praise for every blessing vouchsafed to men. He had a heart for every one; a tear for every woe, and kindly smile for those whose lives had run in pleasant places. He was honored by institutions of learning and highly deserved every honor. He was a Master of Arts, a Doctor of Divinity and a Doctor of Humane Letters. But more than all else he prized the love and esteem of the deaf.

God knows he will be missed by them more and more as time goes by. His helpfulness to the adult deaf can never be measured. But he has gone from us forever, and now, in a house of gloom and sorrow, all that remains of our friend lies in a black–draped casket, and upon his forehead shines the benediction of everlasting peace.

•   •   •

EXCERPTS FROM A SERMON PREACHED AT
A MEMORIAL SERVICE IN
ST. MATTHEW'S CHURCH, N.Y.
BY THE REV. DR. WM. H. VIBBERT, D.D.,
VICAR OF TRINITY CHAPEL, N.Y.,
ON SUNDAY, OCTOBER 26th 1902.

"For David after he had served his own generation by the will of God, fell on sleep."—Acts 13:36.

When I was asked to preach the sermon upon this occasion, and the privilege was offered me of paying my tribute of grateful affection to the memory of my friend whom I had known and loved for many years, these words of St. Paul, which summed up the story of the life of the shepherd-king, came spontaneously into my mind, as the brief but comprehensive biography of our departed father and friend and brother. For truly it may be said of him, "He served his own generation by the will of God, and fell on sleep." In fact, it was said to me a few days ago, by one who knew him well and appreciated his work, " If any man deserved a monument from the people of his own day, it was Dr. Gallaudet." But after all, his life and works are his monument, and his good life stands out fairer than any carved memorial of marble or of brass. A life filled with the enduring fragrance of holy deeds wrought for the love of Christ and the good of man, shining with the gentle ministry of a good example, cheerful and resigned in bright days and dark, "making sunshine in a shady place," perfumed with the incense of self–sacrifice and beautified with the grace of humility, lifts itself as a stately monument on which the finger of grateful love might write the enduring epitaph, "He served his own generation according to the will of God, and fell on sleep." ...

In striving to measure the true greatness of a character like that of our departed brother, we stand perhaps too close to him to get the true perspective of it in its manifold and yet united completeness; our bereaved eyes are too dim to see it in its true proportions. But our loving hearts can comprehend some of its more evident and salient points, which commend it to our love and imitation.

He was above all things, a man of God, a faithful and devoted servant of our Lord and Master, Jesus Christ.

He was a man of prayer, of deep spirituality, which pervaded all his life, into which religion was inwrought as a matter of daily conduct, to enrich it with its charm, and to beautify it with its celestial grace.

He was a man of sympathy, with a tear for every woe, and a smile for every joy.

He was a man of charity, and many of the charities which he dispensed only the manifestation of the last day shall declare, and only the hearts of those who enjoyed his benevolence can tell.

He was a man of lovable tenderness, gentle and gracious in his disposition, bearing benignly in his very face the traits of the character that gave that sweetness to his demeanor and that kindness to his deeds. Large hearted and generous in judgment, he thought of men with inexhaustible compassion and forbearance.

He was a man of enduring patience, of remarkable fidelity, of unwearied perseverance, and of unwavering faith. Though deeply spiritual he was intensely human, and a saving sense of humor kept him from sourness, harshness and discouragement. In the wide range of his work, in the multitude of men with whom he came in contact, in the sphere of his chosen labor, in the generation which he served, the lives he brightened, the souls he cheered, in his untiring devotion to the people of his peculiar care, he won for himself an affection which we may all envy and which we will all do well to emulate. He has left behind him a memory fragrant with the perfume of self-sacrifice, which will live in the hearts of men as a rich and cherished treasure.

And now, he has entered into "the rest that remaineth." Still the world is full of woe and trouble, still the cry of the needy sounds in our ears, still the silent seek our sympathy, and the helpless invoke our aid, still sin stains and blights God's fair creation and darkens human life. These are all calls for our service, for our effort, our sacrifice. It is *our own* day and generation that needs our ministry and requires our service.

Our dear friend will not have lived in vain, if his life, so full of labors for human good, impresses upon us all the duty and the privilege of serving our generation in faithfulness and quietude, without noise or fuss, forgetting self, and making the place where our lot is cast sweeter, happier and better, doing all things according to God's blessed will.

"The night cometh when no man can work." May we, as the shadows gather around us, fall on sleep, in the humble hope that it may be said of us, as we say it, as the best tribute to the memory of our dear departed friend, and as an encouragement to us to follow the Master as he followed Him: "He served his own generation by the will of God, and fell on sleep."

IN MEMORIAM

At a meeting of the pupils, officers and teachers of the Institution (Fanwood), held on the afternoon of Friday, September 26th (1902), the following Minute and Resolutions were adopted:

In the passing away of Reverend Thomas Gallaudet, D.D., L.H.D., we mourn the loss of a friend who performed life-long service for the Institution. From 1843, when, in early manhood, he entered the profession of deaf-mute instruction as a teacher in this Institution, filling a position in this capacity for fifteen years, and subsequently, as a member of the Board of Directors, he ever manifested a warm and constant interest in the work, and loyally did his share to aid its progress and usefulness.

Dr. Gallaudet was elected a Director of the Institution on June 10th, 1862, and served continuously on the Committee of Instruction for forty years. His personal acquaintance with the peculiarities of the deaf child, added to his experience as a teacher in the Institution, and his knowledge of its needs, peculiarly fitted him for a position of so great importance. He was twice elected on the delegations representing the Institution at international congresses of teachers of the deaf, held in Europe, and was frequently the representative of the Directors at the conventions of the American Instructors of the Deaf in this country.

In his capacity as a member of the Committee of Instruction, of which he was Chairman for many years, Dr. Gallaudet was brought into close contact with the pupils, teachers and officers, to all of whom his benevolent countenance was familiar, and with most of whom he was personally acquainted. In his periodic inspection of the school his warm and kindly disposition and his sincerity of purpose became known, to be admired and appreciated; therefore, be it

RESOLVED, That in the death of Dr. Gallaudet the Institution has lost a valued friend whose life-work, closely interwoven in its history and progress, was rich in service;

RESOLVED, That in his death the deaf were left to mourn the loss of a friend of singular sweetness and purity of character, whose life was one of untiring devotion to their uplifting, to the advancement of their education, and of their spiritual and temporal welfare;

RESOLVED, That a copy of this Minute and Resolutions be transmitted to the family of our deceased friend, and that it be presented for publication in the *American Annals of the Deaf* and in the *Deaf–Mutes' Journal* (Oct. 10).

Enoch Henry Currier, Chairman.
Thomas Francis Fox, Secretary.

•   •   •

NEW YORK TIMES EDITORIAL
(Sept. 6, 1902)

Dr. Thomas Gallaudet, a man whose fame extended far beyond national limits, died the other day (Aug. 27) after a long life devoted to the most active sort of labor, and now we learn he left an estate consisting of personal property amounting to $3,000—he had no lands or houses. And Dr. Gallaudet's fame was of the very best sort—that of a man who had benefited, practically and greatly, a considerable number of his fellow human beings, without, as sometimes happens in the case of excellently intentioned benefactions, injuring anybody else in the slightest degree, but, on the contrary, indirectly helping all whom he did not help directly. And at the time of his death, he was "worth," as the saying is, $3,000! Many people will doubtless make this outcome the text for lugubrious sermons, some clerical and some lay, on the wickedness and ingratitude of the whole world and are in the doctor's exiguous fortune clear proof that things are not as they should be—perhaps that they are not as they were in an imaginary period commonly described as "the good old days." As a matter of fact, however, it proves nothing of the kind, but, instead, that life, now as always, and as a rule, gives to men of high desert what they want most and will make them happiest. Certainly Dr. Gallaudet will not have called his career unsatisfactory or made its scanty rewards—in money—an excuse for inveighing against the system of events or their systematizer. Had his ambition been the accumulation of wealth, he would have had a right, after such an expenditure of energy as his, to find fault with fate and criticize his fellows, but early in life he set before himself another object, worked with the best of his ability for its attainment, and—attained it. What more could he or anybody else expect or even want? And, incidentally, he had appreciative recognition all his life from all who knew him and from an infinitely greater number who had heard of him, and even of money itself— to spend in his chosen work—no insignificant amount came into his possession or control. The world is no better than it should be, but it is a pretty decent old world after all.

● ● ●

ADDRESS GIVEN AT ST. ANN'S CHURCH FOR THE DEAF OCTOBER 5 BY THE REV. JACOB M. KOEHLER, VICAR ALL OF SOULS' CHURCH FOR THE DEAF, PHILADELPHIA.

The special topic assigned me presents so many view points that this paper has been prepared with a feeling of some constraint. There are so many things of interest in connection, that even to touch them in passing, would occupy far more than the time allowed.

One has but to read a few of the memorials already published, to realize the strong hold our departed brother had upon the affection and esteem of all who knew him, but especially upon the confidence and love of the deaf community. He was, as one of them has expressed it, "the best beloved and trusted friend of the deaf of this and past generations."

Dr. Gallaudet was completely wrapped up in his work among the deaf. He devoted himself to it with a marvelous generosity, doing with his might whatsoever his hand found to do, with a fervent spirit, serving the Lord. And it was this devotion to their interests that impressed the deaf more than anything else. It was not so much what he *accomplished* as he *tried to do* for them, that attracted their attention and won their love and admiration. All realized the singular simplicity and thorough goodness of his character, and recognized in him a consecrated leader of souls to Christ. No one could spend even a short time in his company without feeling the influence of his simple goodness.

His broad sympathies impressed every one. He was tolerant of all opinions that can be tolerated in the Church, although he held with unquestioned tenacity to her distinctive principles. The remarkable good he accomplished along Church lines, stimulated others "not of this fold" to undertake similar work, sometimes with good results. But while deploring these divisions among a people so few and scattered, Dr. Gallaudet had no quarrel with those who could not work with him in his own way. What *he* did or thought was less for himself than for the silent children of God's family.

"Their welfare pleased him, and their cares distressed,
To them his heart, his hopes, his griefs were given."

His earnest prayer and aim was that all may be found in the ranks of the redeemed.

The gratitude of the deaf towards their benefactors is one of their most noteworthy traits, and it has been exhibited so often as to become almost proverbial; and their grateful appreciation of Dr. Gallaudet's labors was shown in many ways during his life. Among many instances, a few years ago the "Congress of the British Deaf and Dumb" presented him with a beautifully illuminated address; and on the occasion of his golden wedding anniversary in 1895, hundreds gathered from all parts of the country, bringing congratulations and gifts, among the latter a purse of over five hundred dollars of gold. He was always an honored guest at conventions of the deaf, and I recall in particular the great ovation he received at an International Congress held in Paris. It was my privilege to be with him at many gatherings of the deaf here and abroad, and I can testify to the universal respect for him, and the quiet yet forceful influence he exerted everywhere.

The impression Dr. Gallaudet made upon the deaf is best shown, perhaps, in the way they are carrying on his life work. In the Church *nine deaf men have been ordained* who have brought thousands of their fellows into pastoral relations. Their work ramifies into nearly every diocese. Others are preparing themselves for the ministry; and in the denominations several are doing well for the moral and spiritual uplifting of the class. In Ohio, the deaf have for some years maintained a Home for their Aged and Infirm; and those in Pennsylvania will soon open a similar one, in a building not easily duplicated among charitable institutions. Other enterprises of a like character are under way elsewhere, in all of which the deaf themselves are taking a leading part. Can better illustrations be offered of the impression made by Dr. Gallaudet's personality and work upon the deaf community? Can anything better show their filial regard for him?

His death caused universal sorrow among the deaf, and their tributes to his worth are most beautiful and touching. These come from all quarters, and demonstrate with remarkable unanimity the great impression made upon the deaf by Dr. Gallaudet's life—a life which as its beauty and power are unfolded to us, is marked, more and more, as one truly "hid with Christ in God."

To quote from a minute adopted by the "Empire State Association of Deaf–Mutes," at Troy, on the day of Dr. Gallaudet's funeral, "through more than sixty years of loving ministration in their cause, he never swerved in devotion to their interests, so that in his death the deaf at large have been truly bereaved of a benefactor whose good works they revere and whose name they will hold in lasting remembrance." And says *Le Journal des Sourds–Mutes*, of Paris: "If his memory be imperishable among the deaf of America, it is equally so among the deaf of France; for he visited them often, every time giving them evidence of his great goodness."

I think there is no need to enlarge upon the topic. "Ye know after what manner he has been with you at all seasons, serving the Lord with all humility of mind, and how he kept back nothing that was profitable to you, but showed you and taught you publicly and from house to house testifying repentance towards God and faith towards our Lord Jesus Christ."

And, now,

> *"Doubtless unto him is given*
> *A life that bears immortal fruit,*
> *In such great offices as suit*
> *The full-grown energies of Heaven."*

•   •   •

EDITORIAL
The Buff and Blue, vol. 9, no. 2
Student Publication, Gallaudet College.

In the death of this good man (The Rev. Dr. Thomas Gallaudet) the College sustains a distinct loss; for, although he was in no way officially connected with the college, the warmth of his moral atmosphere cheered and inspired generation after generation of students. His frequent visits to his brother, President Gallaudet, and his never failing attendance upon the exercises of Presentation Week established relations between him and the students as a body and as individuals; for, besides speaking to them frequently and feelingly from the platform, it was his habit to go among them and renew acquaintances formed during his visits to state schools, and to seek introductions to those he had not met before. In this way nearly every student in the college was brought within the influence of his singularly attractive and Christlike personality.

It was this personality, more than anything he said, that impressed all who met him. His interlocutors needed no asseverations of his disinterested friendliness; it was written on every feature of his kindly face; it shone from his speaking eyes; it thrilled in his warm and tender hand-clasp. To meet him but for a few moments even was to assure one's self of a friend in sorest need.

And thus he passed among us shedding abroad the love of Christ, a wholesome and restraining influence upon the fiery impatience and passion of youth. Where we looked with anger and hate, he gazed with sorrow and love. Bitter denunciation, the bludgeon, and the sword were not his weapons of reform. His methods were those gentle methods of Christ, and his daily walk and conversation impressed upon us the value of charity, faith, patience, and persistence in the reformation of wrong and the reclamation of the wrong doer,—"Being reviled he blessed, being persecuted he suffered" and "did good to those that despitefully used him" —in all things he was an impressive example of what the human can attain of the divine Christ–like nature, and as such an invaluable beacon to the young in these later days when we are taught that the mailed, not the open, hand is the best missionary of religion and civilization.

He will be missed as a friend and as a restraining, guiding influence; but if we as young people can pattern our lives after his, it will be the tenderest memorial, and the one that would have been the most acceptable to him.

• • •

EULOGY GIVEN AT ST. MATTHEW'S CHURCH, NEW YORK CITY, FRIDAY, AUGUST 29, 1902, BY THE RT. REV. H. C. POTTER, BISHOP OF NEW YORK.

I remember very vividly the first time that I ever saw Dr. Gallaudet. I was a candidate for holy orders. I do not want to say anything to give anybody pain—certainly not a priest of the Church, whose office it is to minister in the City of New York; but I was wandering about the streets of New York on a summer day—it was in August, I remember—to find, if I might, a church that was open on a Sunday afternoon in August. I am sorry to say that I was not very successful, till I came to St. Ann's Church, where I supposed, curiously enough (such was my ignorance) that I had found my way into a church of extreme ritualistic usage, because the priest was standing before the altar in a black gown, in absolute silence, communicating by motions what he had to communicate to the people. Presently I discovered where I was, and soon fell under the spell of what I think nobody who ever saw him failed to recognize, and that was the spell of the singular eloquence—let me say it, my friends, whose office is to communicate the Word of God and the mind of God by human gestures, and not by human speech—the singular grace and beauty and eloquence of Dr. Gallaudet's action as a preacher with the hands, and by signs. Nobody who ever heard him read the service, and knew what a singularly fine organ he had, and with what dignity and stateliness he could make himself heard in any congregation, could be unmindful that he was, as it were, putting one gift upon the shelf, in order that he might use the other for that people to whom he was bound in so many and such tender ways. I have always thought that his consecration of his gifts to their service was one of the finest things in the history of religion in this land.

His father, unless I am mistaken, had been head of the Institution for the Training of Deaf-Mutes in Hartford, and his mother herself was a mute. Now, then, I can well imagine how a man who had grown up in that atmosphere could have turned his back upon it, and felt, at any rate, that if he went into the ministry he would exercise an entirely different group of gifts, and address himself to an entirely different type of congregation. Dr. Gallaudet did not do so. He took up the work among deaf-mutes in this land, and he was a missionary going all over the land.

When I was at Trinity Church, Boston (it is a great joy to remember at this moment), I had the incomparable pleasure of meeting him on Sunday afternoons, for a time, in that dignified church that used to be in Summer Street, when Dr. Gallaudet did me the great honor of translating the very poor sermons which I preached on those afternoons, to the people who cane there to worship and listen. Then I came into the relation which he and I have sustained here in this diocese for nearly twenty years, and in which, let me say in this presence, I never parted from him without a new sense of the singular sweetness, transparency, purity and elevation of his character.

He was a most lovable man, of inexhaustible tenderness, and the rare grace and charm with which he moved his hand was an expression and type of his mind. He could not be harsh—at least I could not conceive of him as harsh. He could not be bitter. And in all of life he had a singular philosophy of vision. He looked at things in a large and lofty way. He judged men with inexhaustible charity. And when we were together, some of us who are here, last spring, in the church of which he was rector, I believe until his death, where the deaf-mutes especially were gathered, in the northern part of the city, I shall never forget that night when we prayed for him; how the atmosphere of tenderness, and a certain quality of hunger of love, brooded in the place, and made the dullest conscious of its presence.

Dr. Gallaudet could easily be differentiated from other men by what he was not; but I prefer to remember what he was; to remember how he moved to and fro among all sorts and conditions of men, making life sweeter because he was part of it and human speech more tender, and our judgments of men more forebearing by the exquisite patience which I sometimes think was the finest note of his character, however imperfectly we imitate and reproduce it.

I thank God for his great ministry; and I beseech you, my brethen, to whom especially he spoke, and to whom especially he lived, carry forward the power of his life by the strong and consistent and ardent faith with which you follow and serve your Master, even as he followed and served his!—*The Silent Missionary* (June 1941).

SUPPLEMENT

Henry Winter Syle.

Henry Winter Syle, M.A.

Friend, Servant, Scholar and Teacher

•

edited from a paper

by

Robert C. Sampson

In the Bicentennial Year of the United States of America, the deaf people of Philadelphia—especially those who are members of that tight little coterie known as the congregation of All Souls' Church for the Deaf—have a very special reason to pause and reflect on the many legacies left to them from the past. For one, this is the year when All Souls' Church for the Deaf observes the centennial of the ordination of the Reverend Henry Winter Syle. He was the first Vicar of All Souls' and what makes this ordination so significant is this: Henry Winter Syle has the unique distinction of being the first deaf man to be ordained to the diaconate and subsequently to the priesthood in the Episcopal Church.

Among the deaf men of the era in which Henry Winter Syle lived, there were many who can be classed as showing the attributes of leadership, intelligence and talent, but in some respects Henry Winter Syle towered high above the best educated deaf men of the time and he might have ranked among the top scholars of the Victorian era had he not elected to withdraw from the world and devote his unusual talents to the service of those who were, like himself, deprived of hearing and who did not possess the strength of character and native intelligence which enabled him to surmount obstacles well known to the deaf people. His life was one long series of unselfish deeds, performed in the face of a continual struggle against ill health and adversity. The obstacles in the path he marked out for himself were many and formidable. Such goals would overwhelm even the above-average and highly motivated person—especially one with a less lofty purpose or inferior courage. He had many opportunities to improve his station in life and his best and closest friends sometimes urged him to give up the impossible and seemingly thankless tasks he had assumed, but he never for a moment wavered from the course he had set for himself. Such was the mettle, determination and spirit of the man.

Had Distinguished Forebears

Henry Winter Syle was born in Shanghai, China, on November 9, 1846. His father was the Reverend Edward Syle, D.D.—many years before, a protege of the late Bishop McIlvaine of the Diocese of Ohio. When the good Bishop was in England in 1835, pleading for the College and Seminary in his Diocese, he sought to secure for it not only means but men willing to prepare themselves for what was then considered as frontier missionary work. In the parish of the Reverend Thomas Mortimer, an eminent clergyman of the Church of England, in Pentonville near London, were four young men willing and ready for this work. Circumstances prevented three of them from going, but one, the youngest of the three, whom Mr. Mortimer called "choice young men," crossed the Atlantic, followed Bishop McIlvaine to Gambier and entered Kenyon College in order to fit himself for the ministry. This was in the fall of 1835. The young Englishman pursued his studies satisfactorily and in due time was admitted to holy orders. He soon caught the missionary spirit and sought work in China. He also served, at one time, as Professor of History and Moral Philosophy in the Imperial University of Japan at Kyoto.

Henry Winter Syle's mother, Jane Mary Winter Davis, was a member of the distinguished Davis family of Maryland—a family noted for political and public servants of the people. She was the daughter of the Reverend Henry Lyon Davis, President of St. John's College at Annapolis, Maryland, and Jean Brown Winter. Her brother, Henry Winter Davis—from whom young Syle took his baptismal name—was a prominent attorney-at-law in the city of Baltimore and United States Senator from Maryland. He was a man known for his learning and patriotism and whose character, as drawn by the Hon. J. A. J. Creswell, his colleague in the Thirty-eighth Congress, presents many points of similarity to that of Henry Winter Syle at his maturity. His mother's cousin was another luminary of the Davis family—Judge David Davis, known for his role as President Abraham Lincoln's manager.

Exhibited A Love for Learning

As a child Henry Winter Syle was a precocious boy and early exhibited an aptitude and love for learning. When only three and a half years old the ladies of the mission where his parents were stationed often asked him to read to them from the Bible. The climate did not agree with his health and when he was four and a half years old his parents sent him to America in charge of a returning missionary. He was received into the family of his mother's aunt, Elizabeth Winter, of Alexandria, Virginia, who took a commanding interest in her grand nephew's advancement and at her death she left him a small sum of money to aid him in his studies.

When young Syle was six years old, adversity struck in the form of a severe attack of scarlet fever. This resulted in a total and permanent damage to the auditory nerve. This common malady of childhood affected young Henry Winter's weakened constitution to the point he never enjoyed good health, but the disease did not impair his mental powers.

In November 1853 he was admitted to the celebrated Mr. Bartlett's Family School for Young Deaf-Mute Children which had moved from the Fiftieth Street locale near the New York Institution in the city proper to a temporary site at Fishkill Landing, a beautiful little village in what is known as "The Highlands," and located on the east bank of the Hudson River opposite Newburg. Mr. David Ely Bartlett, a graduate of Yale University and for twenty-four years an instructor of the deaf at the American Asylum for the Deaf in Hartford and at the New York Institution, was the first educator of the deaf to test the philosophy of admitting deaf children to school at as early an age as their parents were willing to entrust to his care. Young Henry Winter Syle was so far in advance of the other children that, instead of placing him in one of the classes, Mr. Bartlett made him the special charge of his accomplished and beautiful wife, who soon became warmly attached to the talented boy. It is because of this lady's skill as a teacher and her encouragement then and in the future that Mr. Syle ascribes much of his success in his studies.

And as an intriguing vignette of young Henry Winter Syle's childhood years, Mrs. Bartlett has this to say: "He had a mind that began early to investigate. For this purpose he would look through all the books he could find on a given subject and surprise us by the knowledge which he had made his own. Soon after he reached the challenging age of eight he took to soldiering and would tramp for hours over the place with his mimic cap and sword, going through imaginary evolution and contriving, as he said 'the best method of surprising an enemy.' When the Crimean War came and was a household topic, he was a juvenile authority on terms of warfare and siege."

The following incident is an instance of his incisive readiness of thought and reply: One day he was driving with Mr. Bartlett, who turned to him and asked "What are you thinking about?" Young Henry Winter replied laconically, "Something." "Where is something?" "Everywhere." "Where is nothing?" "Nowhere." "What is the difference between something and nothing?" Young Syle reflected for a moment and gave Professor Bartlett the *coup d'etat* of all logical answers: "Anything is the pivot on which the bar which separates something from nothing turns." The good Professor probably drove the rest of the way in silence.

Young Henry Winter soon learned to use signs and to play with the other children but he liked better to get away by himself with a book and it was often necessary to hunt him up and send him out to play for his health's sake. At ten years he began the study of Latin. His fertile mind took readily to the intricate points of construction and when it came to translation it was interesting to see how quickly he would pick out the parts of an involved sentence and translate it into good English.

Until he was twelve, he recited orally but his speech grew more and more indistinct. He became sensitive about this and gave it up altogether. After this his translations were written and showed not only his sense of the language but of the surroundings of the subjects. Sometimes he would bring in oddities picked up in his reading as when reading in Quintus Curtius that Alexander the Great took a fever from bathing in the river Cydnus. He remarked, "Frederick Barbarossa did the same thing." He had even less trouble with Greek than with Latin and digging out roots and derivations was a pleasure to him. In other studies he had an equal facility and it was hard to say in which he did his best work—mathematics or science. He enjoyed history greatly and his retentive memory stored it up. His reading of poetry began early and he never lost the sense of rhythm and his punning upon words shows that he kept the memory of sounds. He also, for all his seriousness, had a humorous side and was quick at witty repartee.

It is probable that living in a world without sound aided him in the concentration of his powers and in that attention which has often been called the secret of memory. It is certain that he had a remarkable ability to recall whatever he had read. He had at times a keen sense of his deprivation but fixed trust and incessant industry were the perfect antidotes for keeping young Henry Winter Syle from brooding over it. It was a serious time with him when he faced his future and realized that to him many doors were closed which opened to other young men of his literary tastes and ambitions. There was, for him, times of painful struggle but it ended in submission to the will and guidance of the Lord in whom he believed and in patient waiting for an open way.

When Mr. Bartlett and his family moved to Hartford in order to accept a position in the school there, young Henry Winter Syle accompanied them and he continued to receive private instruction from Mrs. Bartlett and, when time permitted, aid from Mr. Bartlett. He spent much of his spare time at the American Asylum for the Deaf, which counted among its pupils a large number of unusually bright young men, many of whom have since risen to distinction and fame in the recorded history of deaf "greats." Among them were Professor Amos Draper; H. B. Scannell, a deaf publisher; Professor John B. Hotchkiss; George Wing; Harry Moore, the artist, and others who, though not so well known, were men of marked force of character. These young men looked up to Mr. Syle as their intellectual leader and he appears to have first exercised his talent as an organizer in connection with their literary societies.

Some of us may wonder what Henry Winter Syle did for relaxation or had in the way of a hobby. For one he was fond of browsing around the Institution shops and he learned to handle the tools of several trades. He was especially fond of carpentry and in later years frequently sought relief from his many cares in the exercise of his taste for this hobby.

Henry Winter Syle was confirmed by Bishop Horatio Potter of the Diocese of New York in 1858 at the age of eleven years and this event made young Syle consider himself consecrated to Christ's service.

The nineteenth century, even though it was a fertile period for the genesis of deaf notables, was not an opportune era noted for diverse careers for many young deaf men and women blessed with exceptional talents and skills. Henry Winter Syle faced a similar career crisis in his day and at one time he thought seriously of entering the profession and practice of law, but the advice of his uncle, the Honorable Henry Winter Davis, dissuaded him from following this career. The objection Mr. Davis presented was that his nephew's deprivation of hearing would interfere seriously with a full performance of his duties as an attorney in a court of law.

Enters Trinity College

In the fall of 1863, on the advice of his father who had returned to America, Henry Winter Syle entered Trinity College at Hartford. In June 1864 he passed the annual examinations with such high marks as to be admitted to the further examination for honors and passed the latter *cum honore* in Latin and English. In December of the same year an acute bout with inflammation of the eyes compelled Syle's personal physician to order him to discontinue his studies. Even this temporary respite in his academic career did not reflect on him as he was given an honorable dismissal by President Kerfoot, at one time Bishop of Pittsburgh. A letter written by Professor Hart of Trinity shows the respected esteem young Henry Winter had earned while there: "He was in the class below my own and I knew him intimately. He was highly esteemed, both for his scholarship and for the worth of his character, by the officers and students of the college. I well remember the reputation which he had as a careful, graceful and successful student, easily at the head of his class; and I find, on looking over the college record, that my memory is in accordance with the facts of the case. The average mark given him for his literary work in the freshman year was about nine-tenths of the maximum."

To Washington, Then England

When Henry Winter left Trinity he went to Charleston, Virginia, where his father, whose first wife had died and who had married again, lived. At the start of the Civil War the Syle family moved to Washington, D.C. Young Henry Winter Syle was present at the inauguration of Dr. Edward Miner Gallaudet as the first President of the National Deaf-Mute College (now Gallaudet University) and, not wishing to depend on his father, soon after applied for and secured the position of clerk in the administrative offices of the college where his school pals from Old Hartford,

John B. Hotchkiss and Amos G. Draper, were enrolled as students. He wanted to enter the college as a student, but was dissuaded from doing so by the Reverend Thomas Gallaudet and Richard S. Storrs, who considered him to be too far advanced to benefit much from the courses offered by the college. Since his eye trouble had abated to a satisfactory extent, in July 1867 he departed for England to enroll at Cambridge University. The legacy left him by his great aunt was sufficient to support him for a year and he hoped in that time to win a scholarship that would enable him to matriculate at the University. In October he entered St. John's College in that old University and soon became a marked man among the students and the professors. At the annual examination in June 1868 he ranked a sensational "sixth" in a class of one hundred students—and this with the handicap of poor health. He was also awarded one of the "Exhibitions" founded by Sir Ralph Hare. In the Michaelmas Term of that year young Syle entered another crisis in his life—this time his old adversary—ill health in the form of eye strain, exhaustion and spells of violent headaches which compelled him to discontinue reading for honors in mathematics under the tuition of the Reverend Percival Frost, one of the most eminent mathematicians in Cambridge University. And, to compound the blow, the scholarship he so richly deserved was snatched from him by an ironic twist of fate in the personage of a student who had a prior right to it, of which he had not previously cared to avail himself. All this was a bitter disappointment to young Henry Winter and, exhausted in health and in purse, he relinquished his university career and returned to America in February 1869.

Appointed Instructor at New York School

In March 1869 he received appointment as an instructor in the New York School for the Deaf, and while there, at the encouragement and suggestion of Dr. Isaac Lewis Peet, head of the New York school, Henry Winter Syle prepared himself for the continuation of his studies and ultimate matriculation in an American university. Dr. Peet wrote letters on the subject to Dr. Barnard of Columbia and President Woolsey of Yale. The latter agreed to permit Mr. Syle to enter the class of 1869 as a candidate for the degree of Bachelor of Arts, providing he could show that he was able to pass an examination encompassing four years of the university's undergraduate program. Since his health was improving Henry Winter took the bold and vigorous gamble in obtaining a degree, and finding that the course of study at Yale corresponded to what had been his line of study and reading, he applied to President Woolsey for permission and was admitted by the Yale faculty to examination for a degree. This was a brutal three weeks series of examinations tantamount to facing a battery of academic specialists well versed in their knowledge and expertise in their area of testing. The tests ran from late June right into early July 1869. His proficiency so startled the faculty that it unanimously admitted him to the degree of Bachelor of Arts with the class of 1869 and his success in doing so was the subject of astonished comment by President Woolsey of Yale. And in the words of Miss Irene Marguerite Syle, Henry Winter's only surviving daughter: "Father used to say that the Faculty at Yale told him, 'You can teach us better than we can.'"

While an instructor at the New York School and at the very onset of his career, Henry Winter Syle was given charge of the highest grade of the grammar department and he was subsequently made instructor in natural philosophy and chemistry to the high class. When the collegiate department was established he became professor of these branches of study. Mr. Syle, at that stage in his career, possessed qualities which eminently fitted him to the demanding role of an instructor of the deaf. In addition to the remarkable power and activity of his mind, his scholarship and vast fund of information— ever responsive to any demand he or others might make upon it—he had an unusually clear and full knowledge of the structure of the English language and understood, from his long association with the deaf people, the difficulties they encountered with English and how best to overcome them. He was held in high esteem by the teachers and pupils of the school. Mr. Fort Lewis Seliney, a former teacher had this to say about Mr. Syle's stature as a teacher of the deaf:

"Those who associated with him will remember him with affection. Among an unprecedented array of deaf-mute and semi-mute teachers he easily took the lead. He was a man of ideas. and improvement always followed where he was permitted to suggest. It is conceivable that a mind gifted as was this one, habitually at study and bent upon progress in all things, would in due time have given to the world results in the way of text-books or otherwise of the highest value to the cause in which it was employed."

At Yale and Columbia University

In 1872 he received the degree of Master of Arts in course from Yale University and, in addition to everything else, he commenced a course in Metallurgy in the school of Mines at Columbia College (now Columbia University). During his professional tenure as a member of the academic staff at the New York School—by then he held the position of Professor of Chemistry—Mr. Syle also served as Librarian of the Institution and as a part of his personal research he compiled an original and highly important Register of Pupils Admitted to the New York Institution from 1854 to 1875, a valuable collection of statistics and information which entailed considerable labor on his part.

Marries a Roman Catholic

The year 1872 was also a very special time in his life. He was attracted by the exceptional intelligence, beauty and inborn grace of a young girl—Margaret Jane Flannery—a pupil in the High Class at the New York School—and a Roman Catholic. And according to the records of the Pupil Register, Margaret Jane Flannery was born in Brooklyn, N.Y., on August 20, 1853, the seventh child of Stephen and Hornova Flannery. She had seven brothers and two sisters and only three survived when she was admitted to the New York Institution on September 30, 1862. Her father was a bag maker by occupation. She lost her hearing at the age of five from "convulsions due to fright."—a rather ill-defined cause of deafness and understandable in light of the lack of precise and medical diagnosis and knowledge of causes of deafness in those days. After Margaret Jane Flannery received her diploma of "the highest grade" at the close of the school year in 1872, Henry Winter Syle married her and, as an intriguing sideline to this romantic action, her father immediately disowned her for the action of marrying a Protestant!

Sets Up Adult Education Program

Henry Winter Syle did not neglect his religious activities while he was a teacher at the New York Institution. He was very active in the affairs of St. Ann's Church for the Deaf and he assisted the Reverend Dr.Thomas Gallaudet by serving as head of the Bible Class at St. Ann's. In 1874 he resigned from his post as teacher at the New York School in order to open and conduct Mr. Syle's Free Evening Class for Deaf-Mutes. This was a collaborative effort undertaken by him and the Reverend Dr. Gallaudet. The class started in November 1874 under the auspices of the Board of Education of the city of New York. This is possibly the first documented instance of an adult education program set up for the deaf people of the city. It was technically a class of the evening school held in Grammar School No. 40 on East Twenty-Third Street and, while nominally under the principal of that school, Mr. Syle had sole control and direction of the program. The classes were held on three evenings a week from six-thirty to nine. The students under him had partly received previous instruction and were working people. They were, however, deficient in some points of great practical importance to them in their trades and other business— especially in the area of mechanical drawing, bookkeeping and language. Some of them were Germans who came to Mr. Syle to acquire a knowledge of English. His stay in New York was limited, for in December 1874 he received a desirable appointment in the Assay Department of the United States Mint at Philadelphia. In

January 1875 Mr. Syle resigned from the direction of the class and was succeeded by Mr. James S. Wells, a graduate of the New York Institution and a former instructor in the Texas School for the Deaf. However, the Free Class did not prosper as attendance diminished and in 1878 the program was discontinued.

In Employ of United States Mint

With the acceptance of the position of assayer in the Unites States Mint at Philadelphia—a position Henry Winter Syle felt was more to his liking—his residence in New York ended and the Philadelphia chapter opens. The deaf people of Philadelphia soon appreciated the blessing of his presence among them. His deeply religious temperament and upbringing naturally led him to a deep and sincere involvement in the church services for the deaf people in Philadelphia. At that time services were held monthly or oftener by the periodic visitations of the Reverend Dr. Thomas Gallaudet, Rector of St. Ann's Church for the Deaf of New York City. The Philadelphia visitations had their origin when Dr. Gallaudet requested permission of the Diocese of Pennsylvania and of the Reverend Dr. Duchachet, then Rector of St. Stephen's Church at Tenth Street between Market and Chestnut, to conduct services for the deaf Philadelphians. The first service was conducted by the Reverend Dr. Gallaudet on Friday evening, March 4, 1859, in what was then known as the Sunday School Room of the Parish Building at St. Stephen's; about fifty people were present.

When in the employ of the United States Mint, Mr. Syle used his leisure time in the study of theology and within a short time he so thoroughly prepared himself that he was licensed by Bishop William Bacon Stevens as a layreader. He conducted weekly services on the interim Sundays when the Reverend Dr. Gallaudet was not in Philadelphia. Mr. Syle also conducted a Bible class at St. Stephen's.

Ordained A Deacon in 1876

On July 1, 1875, Mr. Syle was admitted as a candidate for Holy Orders by the Bishop and the Standing Committee of Pennsylvania, and by a fortuitous and striking coincidence he received, on the same day, the honorary degree of Master of Arts *ad eundem* from Trinity College, Hartford, Connecticut—the college where he started his college education. He attended the Philadelphia Divinity School and also received personal instruction and attention from the Reverend Thomas Gallaudet. A little more than a year after Mr. Syle was received as a candidate for Holy Orders he was ordained a deacon. He could have been ordained in June 1876, at the end of the twelve months usually required after admission, but for various reasons it seemed better to fix a day in October for the ordination. At the time the Right Reverend William Bacon Stevens, Bishop of the Diocese of Pennsylvania, especially desired to have this particular ordination be as emphatic as possible. Sunday, the eighth of October, 1876, was chosen as the date for Mr. Syle's ordination since it was the Sunday before the annual meeting of the Diocese's Board of Missions and, in addition, many Bishops and prominent clergymen would be in Philadelphia; also it would be more convenient for the deaf people—especially those who wished to visit the Centennial. So on Sunday, October 8, 1876, in St. Stephen's Church, before a large congregation which included five Bishops and many other notable clergymen, Henry Winter Syle was ordained a deacon in the Episcopal Church. Bishop Stevens, in an eloquent and convincing sermon, upheld the validity of the sacraments as administered in the language of signs and announced that, after long and careful study, he had arrived at the conclusion that nothing in the Bible or in the canons of the Church forbade the admission of deaf persons to the priesthood. This was in answer to those who opposed Mr. Syle's ordination as a violation of the principle that men who aspired to office in the Church should be physically as well as mentally sound and perfect, and because they believed that the sacraments of the Holy Communion and of baptism would, if administered without the oral accompaniment of the proper words, be invalid and void. Bishop Stevens' decision was doubtless influenced by Mr. Syle's able and brilliant exposition of the fallacy of these objections and it is, therefore, to Mr. Syle, our present-day deaf clergy owe a debt of thanks for opening to them this profession. The Reverend Dr. Thomas Gallaudet had the honored privilege of presenting Mr. Syle and for the benefit of about sixty deaf people in the assembled congregation the entire service and ordination ceremony was interpreted for them in the language of signs by the Reverend Dr. Francis J. Clerc, the son of the famed deaf instructor, Laurent Clerc, who was instrumental, along with Thomas Hopkins Gallaudet, in establishing the foundations of education of the deaf in the United States. The Reverend Dr. Gallaudet also served as relief interpreter for the Reverend Dr. Clerc when called upon.

And soon after his ordination Mr. Syle was enlisted as one of the assistants to the Reverend William Rudder, D. D., the Rector of St. Stephen's. For a time he continued to work at the United States Mint and gave his Sundays in service of the Philadelphia Protestant Episcopal Deaf-Mute Mission at St. Stephen's. From December 1878 to the end of February 1880 Henry Winter Syle was disabled by his old adversary—ill health—and his church services were maintained by various agencies and the thoughtful assistance of the Reverend Dr. Thomas Gallaudet. In spite of his health problems Mr. Syle commenced to exercise his many duties. At the time Bishop Stevens, with his keen interest in the Deaf-Mute Mission, felt that the work should be broadened out of the confines of just a parochial mission and because of his philosophy on this, the matter was brought before the Diocesan Convention of 1878 and finally on May 15, 1880, the Convention authorized the Bishop to appoint a Commission on Church Work Among Deaf-Mutes.   This action finally conferred on the Reverend Mr. Syle the official designation of Missionary to the Deaf of the Diocese of Pennsylvania.

Goes to England in 1880

Mr. Syle, with the approval of Bishop Stevens, then Chairman ex-officio of the Commission, sailed for Europe on July 10, 1880, to recuperate from the ravages of ill health. While overseas he gained valuable information on mission work among the deaf of England, Scotland and Ireland. He returned to the United States with his health much improved and resumed his pastoral duties. However, he was also compelled to return, on a part-time basis, to his secular work at the United States Mint, and this because of insufficient funds collected by the Diocese at that time—a situation all too familiar, even in this day and age, to some of our clergymen who labor in the vineyard of the specialized ministry to the deaf people and are compelled to fatten lean pay checks with part-time or even full-time secular work. Fortunately for Mr. Syle, the money situation was happily rectified by an inflow of larger contributions and the new-found Diocesan Commission was spared the ignominy and potential disgrace of inability to meet its commitment to the mission work among the deaf people. And because of this, on December 1, 1880, he formally terminated his part-time employment at the United States Mint.   In addition to his many duties he also served as chaplain of the Philadelphia Literary Association of Deaf-Mutes— later known as the Clerc Literary Association.

A very assertive characteristic of the Reverend Henry Winter Syle was this—the higher he rose above the deaf people, the more he gave of himself to their needs and interests and his gradual advance from grade to grade in church preferments was not lost on Bishop Stevens. Mr. Syle pushed aggressively to extend the work throughout the diocese and beyond its confines through the authorization of neighboring dioceses such as New Jersey, Delaware and Maryland. His role as "circuit rider" took him on monthly visits to Baltimore, Washington, Frederick and occasionally to Trenton, but the main focus was placed on his work in Philadelphia and neighboring Camden. At. St. Stephen's his work was recorded as a "mission of St. Stephen's," for which the Reverend Mr. Syle received an annual salary of four hundred dollars.

Syle And Mann Ordained Priests

On October 14, 1883, at the Church of the Covenant on Filbert Street, the Reverend Mr. Syle and the Reverend Mr. Mann were ordained Priests in the Episcopal Church by the Right Reverend William Bacon Stevens. This event made them the first deaf men to be admitted to the sacred office as far as is known. After this, Reverend Henry Winter Syle devoted the vast energies of his mind to widen and improve the work of the Church Mission to the Deaf-Mutes. He organized the first "Guild" or religious society of the deaf—The Ephphatha Guild. It had for its primary goal the duty to go into every level of the deaf society of the time and provide, here and there, the necessary assistance to the deaf people in their hour of need. The Guild also started in 1878 a modest fund drive aimed at building a Church for the deaf people of Philadelphia. At the time it had a modest two hundred and fifty dollars and the Literary Society also had a sum of five hundred and fifty dollars to be used for a Hall in the future Church. At a meeting of the Diocesan Commission on May 20, 1881, the Commission gave its blessing and sanction to the deaf people in their effort to raise funds to build a church of their own in Philadelphia.

The mission work in Philadelphia, at St. Stephen's, continued to progress until May 1885, when the connection with that parish ended. The urban sprawl and rapid extension of the city of Philadelphia combined with the miserable public transportation of the time—a situation which is a common malaise even today—prevented many deaf church-goers from regular attendance at the Sunday services. Mr. Syle, long aware of the problem, finally had the Sunday services and meetings transferred to the Church of the Convenant on Filbert Street. The deaf congregation, their Guild and societies moved *en masse* and remained at the Church of the Covenant as guests of that parish until the building was sold in 1887. This action returned the congregation to St. Stephen's—this time simply as guests of the church.

In 1887 the Reverend Henry Winter Syle, sensing that the Mission could never prosper in borrowed quarters or on the "as our guest" terms, advanced a bold project to plan a church exclusively for the deaf people in Philadelphia. The two thousand dollars painfully saved up by the Guild and the Literary Association went down the drain when the money was used for improvements at the Calvary Monumental Church where the congregation had its services for a time. Mr. Syle's scheme was looked upon by many in the deaf congregation with skepticism and classed as a "wild and way-out proposition," but the first contribution of twenty-five cents, made by an old deaf lady—a Mrs. M. A. Paullin—started the ball rolling in the fund-raising. Mr. Syle, being the patient soul he was, continued his devoted labors and efforts to build up his congregation. Twenty-five years previous, the church had no communicants among the deaf and by the time of the twenty-fifth anniversary of the Philadelphia Church Mission to the Deaf-Mutes—celebrated in March 1884— Philadelphia had an active congregation of eighty-two deaf people; one hundred had been baptized and more than a hundred confirmed—a striking testimonial to the Reverend Mr. Syle's magnetic charisma in getting people involved in the Church.

The persistent and tenacious efforts of the patient missionary, plus the slow-but-sure efforts of the Guild, the Literary Society, and some of the more influential friends of the deaf people, finally brought in generous contributions and, at length, a timely gift of five-thousand dollars under the will of Miss Catherine M. Bohlen and the donation of a thousand dollars from the Society for the Advancement of Christianity in Pennsylvania brought the "wild" project out of the dream stage and into the realm of practical reality. On July 12, 1888, a building located on Franklin Street above Green originally the First Cumberland Presbyterian Church and subsequently the Jewish Synagogue Beth El Emeth—was purchased for nine thousand dollars, and a further sum of four thousand was spent to put the building into an acceptable shape as a place of worship for the deaf congregation of the Philadelphia Church Mission to the Deaf-Mutes.

Church For the Deaf Consecrated

On Saturday morning, December 8, 1888, the new church was formally consecrated by Bishop Whitaker, successor to Bishop Stevens, and the church was given the name of All Souls' Church for the Deaf; the Reverend Henry Winter Syle was installed as its pastor. One of the first public services in the new church was the fifth convention of the Conference on Church Work Among the Deaf. It took another year to get up enough money to complete appropriate alternations before the church could be used regularly for Sunday evening worship.

The Reverend Mr. Syle did not confine himself to the religious instruction of the deaf. He also interested himself avidly in their temporal welfare, both as a class and individuals. The Clerc Literary Association, All Souls' Working People's Club and other organizations which met at the new Church always found in him a wise counselor and advocate. He was at his best as an organizer, and as testimonial to his efficiency in perfecting organizations many of them persist to this day. He could always be relied on for advice and assistance in time of trouble. Even those living in New Jersey and Delaware would travel long distances to consult with him on their personal problems. He never asked their creed, and his aid was as freely given to those who opposed his church as to his own parishioners, to those who reviled him as to those who were his warmest friends. His salary as missionary was not large; yet, although he never boasted of his charities, it was known that a great part of it went to relieve cases of destitution. Often his benefits were rewarded with the basest ingratitude, but this never affected his actions no matter how much it wounded his feeling. He was almost sublime in the patience and charitableness with which he endured the many petty persecutions and annoyances to which he was subjected. This is very evident when one takes the trouble to peruse the minute books of organizations such as the Clerc

Literary Organization. The C.L.A., as it is known today, was the "stormy petrel" of organizations of the deaf in Philadelphia and still is to this day. There were times when even Mr. Syle's patience was sorely tried, and at one time he even threatened to resign from the Clerc Literary Association. Organizations were run with a rigidity unheard of today and the inflexibility of organizational rules were such that members were expelled with periodic regularity for petty infractions or fined five cents for absences without an excuse short of being desperately ill!

Four Children Born to Syles

Little is known of the Reverend Henry Winter Syle's family life beyond the information that he and his devoted wife Margaret Jane Syle had four children—Edward Bushrod Syle, named after his great grandfather who is said to have owned the farm where the United States Capitol today stands; Walter Dupont Syle, named after a Dupont who was a close friend of the family; Herbert Bacon Syle, so named after the Bishop who ordained Henry Winter Syle to the diaconate and priesthood, and Irene Marguerite Syle. Of the four, only Miss Irene M. Syle[*] survives today. Among the treasured possessions in All Souls' Church for the Deaf is a faded photograph which depicts the charm and whimsy of a world long gone by—an era known as La Belle Epoque. The photograph, in All Souls' possession, shows the Reverend Mr. Syle, his faithful Margaret Syle and three of their children out on a Sunday stroll. Photographs are a record of things frozen in time and do not tell us much about people and their personalities. However, we do know that the Reverend Mr. Syle was a frail, slight-built man somewhat below medium in height. His face, according to

[*] Miss Irene M. Syle undoubtedly provided much information about her father for this article, which was first written up by Mr. Robert C. Sampson of Old Greenwich, Conn., and then edited by the Centennial Committee of All Souls' Church for the Deaf, Philadelphia—observed in 1976. Miss Syle died in 1978 at the age of 88 years. Her remains are interred near the grave of her parents in West Laurel Hill Cemetery in the Bala Cynwyd area of Philadelphia.

recorded comments of his friends and contemporaries, bore traces of constant suffering. He had a chronic inflammation of the tissues of his brain, which frequently caused him intractable pain through spells of violent headaches. This condition so effected his mind that at one time he requested hospitalization. Even when these headaches were at their worst, it was only necessary to bring up a subject in which he had a keen interest and he would immediately draw himself up out of the prone position and be at once alive with suggestions, arguments and ideas. He was a brilliant conversationalist when in the company of those who could appreciate him and at such times there would flow from his fingers a sparkling stream of witticisms and humorous anecdotes which amused without offending or shocking anyone. He was a good listener and often availed himself of the constructive ideas and suggestions of others. He was, for a man in his position, remarkably free of the cardinal vices of conceit or self-assertion. He was a clear, rapid and very graceful signmaker with the facility of saying much in a few simple sentences.

A Versatile Writer and Editor

When it came to his personal talents his predominant characteristic was the minuteness and perfection with which he did everything he undertook. He even had the "built-in" habit of editing printed reports and inserting personal comments along the margins of printed pages. His versatility as a writer was legendary and this can be gleaned from a very prolific list of his literary efforts—the majority of which have appeared at various times in the *American Annals of the Deaf*, today the oldest professional journal in the United States. Much of his literary efforts on behalf of the deaf people were prepared for the *Deaf-Mutes' Journal*, of which, because of his fluency in five languages, he was Foreign News Editor from 1875 to 1877. Incidentally, another of Henry Winter Syle's curious habits was his penchant for doing letters to his brother in classic Latin or Greek. He began in November 1887 the publication of a monthly sixteen-page periodical with the help of the Reverend Jacob M. Koehler as associate editor. This periodical was originally called the *Silent Catholic*, but as the name gave rise to misunderstandings, it was rechristened the *Silent Missionary*, and it exists today as the *Deaf Episcopalian* under the "imprimatur" of the Episcopal Conference of the Deaf, formerly the Conference of Church Workers Among the Deaf. He also contributed numerous papers which were read before the Empire State Association of Deaf-Mutes and the Pennsylvania Society for the Advancement of the Deaf.

During his tenure on the academic staff at the New York Institution he prepared a Catalogue of Works in the New York Institution Library. He assisted Dr. Edward Allen Fay, editor of the *American Annals* and one of the all-time greats in education of the deaf, in the preparation of the first Index to the *American Annals of the Deaf*, covering volume I through XX and the years 1847 through 1875. The Reverend Mr. Syle also prepared an article on the deaf for Appleton's American Cyclopaedia, which was published in 1873-1874. His magnificent "A Retrospect of Education of the Deaf" was published as an *avant-courier* of the work and it contained priceless engravings done by William R. Cullingworth, a faithful member of All Soul's congregation and in his own right a very skilled engraver. The pamphlet was prepared for the Clerc Centennial Commemoration, which was celebrated on December 28, 1885.

Last Things

The Reverend Henry Winter Syle's last public appearance was at the sixth convention of the Conference of Church Workers Among the Deaf-Mutes held at St. Ann's Church for the Deaf in New York City in October of 1889. It was the last time he celebrated the Holy Communion in that Church. Many who witnessed the vigor with which the Reverend Mr. Syle discussed church affairs little realized that before six months were up his work on earth would be completed.

Although troubled for some time with the prevailing ailment "la grippe" he was busily engaged in a campaign for a home for aged and infirm deaf persons, which materialized at Doylestown, Pennsylvania, in 1902—after his death. His friends who were aware of his illness were quite concerned as they knew of his frail constitution and that he had recently overexerted himself in connection with preparations for the De l'Epée celebration and certain church affairs. He was progressing favorably when, anxious to attend to his work, he left his sickbed to be about his church duties. The January weather was damp and disagreeable and within a day he came down with a high fever, which ended in an acute attack of influenza followed by pneumonia. Even when tossing in delirium during his final illness his mind was filled with plans for the benefit of the deaf people of Philadelphia who were his special charge and every lucid moment was used in giving directions for the carrying on of his work. Finally, at six-thirty on the evening of January 6, 1890— the Epiphany—the Reverend Henry Winter Syle quietly passed away in his home at 2143 Mount Vernon Street.

The news of the death of this brilliant and devoted pastor of All Souls' Church for the Deaf did not pass unnoticed. His role as an organizer and staunch advocate of the deaf people was in every newspaper in Philadelphia; even these in other cities carried obituaries about this most remarkable of deaf men.

On the afternoon of January 9, 1890, the little Church on Franklin Street above Green—a firm testimonial of the brief but determined efforts of its late pastor—was the scene of a funeral service conducted by the Reverend J. Andrews Harris, Rector of St. Paul's Church of Chestnut Hill, and interpreted for the benefit of the deaf congregation by the Reverend Dr. Thomas Gallaudet of New York City. The Reverend Henry Winter Syle was buried at West Laurel Hill Cemetery in the suburb of Philadelphia known as Bala Cynwyd. He spent but a brief time in his chosen work but he left an enduring legacy in the organizations within All Souls' Church for the Deaf and they persist to this day. In the words of his astute mentor and friend, Bishop William Bacon Stevens—"He hath done all things well."

APPENDIX

A. Austin Ward Mann
B. John Carlin
C. Dr. Thomas Gallaudet
   at Philadelphia

SECTION A.

TENTH ANNUAL REPORT

OF

Church Work Among Deaf-Mutes

IN THE

CENTRAL WESTERN AND NORTH WESTERN DIOCESES.

BY

REV. A. W. MANN,

GENERAL MISSIONARY.

Rev. Austin W. Mann

PREFACE

For the first time this report, dating from July 1st, 1884, to July 1st, 1885, is published in a pamphlet by itself. In the past, my reports have been published in the Appendix of the Reports of the Eastern Society. Portions of this, as well as future ones, will be published there, for the sake of the general interest promoted by publishing reports from all departments together. But as a means of promoting a local interest, the reports of work in the Central Western and North Western Dioceses may well be published in full hereafter, separately.

                                                          A. W. Mann

82 Woodland Court
Cleveland, O., July 1st, 1885.

HISTORY

After the establishment of the school for the deaf-mutes at Hartford, Conn., in 1817, similar schools sprang up in somewhat close succession in different parts of the Union. In the course of a score of years, their graduates had increased to a large number. They were scattered, one here, one there, widely apart; and were without spiritual care. They could not join in divine worship with their hearing brethen, except where the Prayer Book was used. But they received no benefit from the oral presentation of the gospel, nor from the soul-stirring strains of music.

It became evident, then, that they needed the Church's services in the living, graceful language of signs, which is to them the most effective substitute for the tones of the voice.

It was not until the year 1850 that steps were undertaken towards meeting the spiritual needs of these long neglected people. The Rev. Thomas Gallaudet, D.D., formed a bible class of deaf-mutes in New York City. Two years later, St. Ann's Church for deaf-mutes sprang into existence as an outgrowth.

For years this interesting work was necessarily limited to the metropolis. Its influence, however, extended widely. Many were the requests coming from afar from the deaf-mutes for the Prayer Book services in their own language; requests that could not be met often, owing to the engrossing parochial duties of Dr. Gallaudet, which were of a dual character, he having a hearing congregation, as well as deaf-mutes, under his spiritual care.

In the year of 1872, the society known as the Church Mission to Deaf-Mutes was organized, with the object of meeting in a systematic way the growing demand. Its work is now limited to the Dioceses of New York, Albany, Northern New Jersey and New England. Its affairs are managed by Dr. Gallaudet, who retains his connection with St. Ann's Church, as Rector. His assistants are the Rev. John Chamberlain, and the Rev. Anson T. Colt, and two or three lay readers. His father founded the school at Hartford, to which reference has just been made.

This new work of the Church, having grown extensively from a small beginning, is now divided into several departments, one of which has just been described. The others are briefly referred to below:

The Rev Francis J. Clerc, D.D., Rector of St. Paul's Church, Philipsburg, Diocese of Central Pennsylvania, ministers occasionally to the deaf-mutes of the Diocese and outside. His father was associated with the elder Gallaudet in the establishment of the school at Hartford; and was instrumental in organizing the school at Philadelphia, in 1820. Mr. J. M. Koehler, a deaf-mute candidate for Holy Orders, is doing excellent itinerary work in this Diocese.

The spiritual interests of the deaf-mutes of Philadelphia and vicinity are ministered unto by the Rev. Henry Winter Syle, M. A., a deaf-mute in Priest's Orders. His work has been most successful. A building fund for a church and mission house is being raised.

Rev. Job Turner traverses several of the Southern States, holding occasional services.

The Rev. Thomas B. Berry, Rector of Christ Church, Guilford, N.Y., ministers occasionally to the deaf-mutes of the Dioceses of Central and Western New York.

THE WORK IN THE CENTRAL WESTERN AND NORTH WESTERN DIOCESES

In 1875, the writer took charge of the work in the Dioceses of Pittsburgh, Ohio, Southern Ohio, Indiana, Michigan, Western Michigan, Chicago, Springfield, Quincy, Missouri, Iowa, Minnesota, Fond du Lac and Wisconsin. The work is of an itinerary character exclusively, as the following diary shows. Within this extensive field about 9,000 deaf-mutes reside, of whom about 3,000 are reached.

The summary at the end of this diary shows the results of the labor of ten years.

DIARY

July, 1884

1st. Returning home from Indiana, I found a good sized mail. 2nd and 3d. Busy answering letters and preparing quarterly reports. 4th. Spent the day quietly at home, writing some. At 5 o'clock Rev. Dr. Gallaudet arrived from New York. At 6:30 P.M. we left Cleveland together for the Northwest. Saturday, 5th. Spent most of the day with the deaf-mutes of Chicago and vicinity, at a picnic. Sunday, 6th. After morning service at St. James' Church, Chicago, we dined with the Rector, Rev. Dr. Vibbert. At 3 o'clock P.M. we held a service for deaf-mutes only, at St. James' Church; and at 8 o'clock P.M. we held a service at the Cathedral, assisted by the Rev. J. H. Knowles. Bishop McLaren was present. Two deaf-mutes received baptism. 7th. Combined service at St. Paul's Church, Milwaukee, Rector, the Rev. C. S. Lester. I baptized a child of deaf-mute parents. Leaving at midnight, we reached St. Paul at noon of the 8th. Before going to Faribault, we called on the Rev. M. N. Gilbert, Rector of Christ Church, to arrange the details of a combined service to be held next week. 9th. Faribault, attending a national conference of deaf-mute schools, at the Minnesota School for the Deaf. On the first day of the session we had the pleasure of meeting Bishop Whipple at St. Mary's Hall, and having a brief consultation concerning Church work among the deaf of the Diocese. 11th. A combined service was held at the Cathedral of Our Merciful Savior, at 8 o'clock P.M. Saturday, 12th. We left the conference, and went to St. Paul. During our sojourn at Faribault we were hospitably entertained at St. Mary's Hall, by the Rev. Geo. B. Whipple, Dean of the Cathedral. Sunday, 13th. Dr. Gallaudet preached for Rev. Dr. Thomas of St. Paul's Church, St. Paul. At 3 o'clock P.M., we held a service for deaf-mutes only at Gethsemane Church, Minneapolis; and a combined service at 8 o'clock, assisted by the Rev. A. R. Graves, the Rector. I baptized an adult deaf-mute. Monday, 14th, morning, Minneapolis, I baptized a sick child of deaf-mute parents at a house. Evening, combined service at Christ Church, St. Paul, the Rev. M. N. Gilbert assisting. Met several delegates of the conference, which adjourned at Faribault this morning. Tuesday, 15th, we conducted a combined service at St. Paul's Church, Winona. Wednesday, 16th. Reached Madison, Wis., at noon. A national convention of educators was in session. Several of the delegates of the Faribault conference were present. Prof. A. G. Bell read a lengthy paper, which was replied to very ably by Prof. Gordon, of the National Deaf-Mute College. The discussion which followed bore upon the merits of the three systems of deaf-mute education— the oral, the manual, and that combining both. It was interesting to note that the weight of testimony of the ablest and most experienced educators was in favor of retaining sign, or manual language as a more rapid and satisfactory means of educating the majority of deaf-mutes. 17th. A combined service was held in the evening at Grace Church, with the assistance of the Rev. Fayette Durlin, Rector. During our stay in this beautiful city we were the guests of Mrs. Chittenden. Left Madison late in the night. 18th. Changed cars in the morning at Chicago, and reached Cleveland after a hot and uncomfortable ride all day. 19th, Cleveland. We called on Gen. Devereux, Mr. Lewis Williams, and other friends. Sunday, 20th, Cleveland. 10:30 A.M., Dr. Gallaudet preached for Rev. Mr. Clendenin, Rector of Grace Church, while I conducted a service for deaf-mutes only in the chapel adjoining. My congregation was dismissed in time for the communicants to receive the Holy Communion in the Church. 3 P. M. Service for deaf-mutes only at Grace Church; and a combined service in the evening at St. John's Church, the Rev. C. S. Bates, D.D., minister in charge. 21st. Dr. Gallaudet left for New York. I was busy with an accumulated mail and a new schedule of appointments. 22nd. Went with my family to Medina, Ohio. 23d, 24th, 25th, at Medina. 26th Went to Pittsburgh. Sunday, 27th. At 3 P. M., conducted a service for deaf-mutes at Trinity Church, the Rev. Samuel Maxwell, Rector. 28th, Returned to Medina, via Cleveland. 29th, All day at Medina. 30th and 31st. At Cleveland, busy with my mail and the preparation of an address.

August

1st and 2d. Busy writing; made some calls. Sunday, 3d. Conducted two services at Grace Church, Cleveland, and distributed several Prayer Books. 4th. Family returned from Medina. Put into the printer's hands the manuscript of a brief appeal for offerings on the Twefth Sunday after Trinity. 5th and 6th. Busy mailing these appeals to the Rectors. 7th. A man called on me about getting his deaf-mute boy into school at Columbus, O. 8th and 9th. My family left for West Virginia. I went to Cincinnati. Sunday, 10th. Conducted service at 3 P.M., at St. Paul's Church, the Rev. Dr. Benedict, Rector. Monday, 11th. Conducted a service at Christ Church, Dayton, Ohio. Tuesday, 12th. Service at Trinity Church, Columbus. Guest of the State Institution. Wednesday, 13th. Joined in the bonds of holy matrimony Mr. J. H. V. Fowler and Miss M. L. Baxter, in one of the parlors of the Institution. Returned to Cleveland in the evening. 14th. Alone at home and quite busy writing. Received 200 annual reports from New York. 15th. Occupied as yesterday. 16th. Departed for St. Louis in the afternoon. Sunday, 17th. Conducted service, at 3 o'clock P. M.. at Christ Church, Rev. Dr. Schuyler, Rector. 18th. Returned home, and commenced correspondence relating to a trip through Indiana, Illinois and Iowa, with the Rev. John Chamberlain. 19th, 20th, 21st and 22d. Preparing an address to be delivered at Peru, Indiana, and a new series of appointments. 23d. Went to Detroit. Called on several friends. Sunday, 24th. Conducted service at St. John's Church, at 10:30 A. M. At 3 o'clock P. M., I attended the Sunday School of Grace Church, and, at the expressed desire of the children, gave sign renditions of the Lord's Prayer, Creed and the Hymn "Nearer, My God, to Thee." At 8 o'clock P. M., a combined service was held in Grace Church with the assistance of the Rector, The Rev. Dr. McCarroll. Monday, 25th. Combined service at Grace Church, Sandusky, Ohio, with the assistance of the Rector, the Rev. F. K. Brooke. 26th. Returned home in the morning. My family returned from West Va., in the afternoon. 27th. Giving a little further attention to the coming tour with the Rev. Mr. Chamberlain, who arrived on the following day. Friday, 29th. Left home with the Rev. Mr. Chamberlain. We reached Peru, Ind., in the afternoon, and went to the hotel. 30th. Attending a reunion of deaf-mutes at the fair ground, near the city. Sunday, 31st. Two combined services at the grounds, at 10:30 o'clock A.M. and 3 o'clock P.M., and another at Trinity Church in the evening. The Church was filled to its utmost capacity.

September

Monday, 1st. Rev. Mr. Chamberlain and I reached Michigan City, Ind., in the afternoon. Rev. Mr. Faude, Rector of Trinity Church, met us at the station and took us to the residence of Mr. Barker, where we were hospitably entertained. In the evening a service was held at Trinity Church. 2d. Service at St. James' Church, Chicago, with a large congregation of deaf-mutes. 3d. Combined service at Christ Church, Joliet, Ill., assisted by the Rev. Mr. Jewell, the assistant minister. 4th. Having cancelled the appointment for Wilmington, we went to Chicago, and spent the day there. 5th. Combined service at St. Luke's Church, Dixon, Illinois, assisted by the Rector, the Rev. John Wilkinson. 6th. Left Dixon at past midnight, and reached Cedar Rapids, Iowa, early in the morning, to attend a convention of the graduates of the Iowa Institution. In the evening we took tea at the rectory. Sunday, 7th. Combined service at Grace Church at 10:30 A. M., assisted by the Rev. Dr. Ringgold. Rev. Mr. Chamberlain made the address. At 4 P. M., a service for deaf-mutes only was held, by Rev. Mr. Chamberlain and myself at Grace Church. At 7:30 P. M. another combined service was held at the mission across the river assisted by the Rev. Dr. Ringgold. Our congregations were large. Monday, 8th. Attended the first session of the convention, and made a few remarks. The day was extremely hot. 9th. I left Cedar Rapids early in the morning, and with the assistance of Rev. R. F. Sweet, conducted a combined service at Trinity Church, Rock Island. Rev. Mr.

Chamberlain went to Council Bluffs. 10th. After a tedious trip, I reached home at nearly midnight. 11th. Busy with a good sized mail. Several Ephphatha returns were acknowledged. 12th. Wrote 55 letters and postal cards today. 13th. Busy preparing for services to-morrow. Sunday, 14th, Cleveland, O, Conducted a service in the Chapel of Trinity Church. 15th and 16th. Busy at home. 17th. Left for Joliet, Illinois, 18th. Joliet. Solemnized marriage between Mr. Julius G. Krafft and Miss Agnes Maria Sartori. Left Joliet in the evening. 19th. Reached Columbus, O., in the morning. Called at the Institution before going home. 20th. Mailed a number of letters before leaving home. Sunday, 21st. Attended morning worship at Trinity Church, Pittsburgh, and held a service in the chapel in the afternoon. 22d. Made a few calls in Pittsburgh before returning home in the evening. 23d and 24th. Closely at my desk at home. 25th. Joined in the bonds of holy matrimony Mr. August Helwig and Miss Rosa Kupfer. Rev. Mr. Chamberlain arrived from the west at night. 26th. Had a very pleasant visit and consultation with him. He left for New York. Sunday 28th. St. Louis. Conducted a service at Christ Church at 3 o'clock P. M. 29th. Left St. Louis at 7:30 A. M. Reaching Indianapolis, I called to see Bishop Knickerbacker, but he was out of the city. I then called on the Rev. E. A. Bradley, D.D. In the evening I held a service at Christ Church. 30th. Went to Jeffersonville and held a combined service at St. Paul's Church, with the Rev. J. R. Bicknell. Before the service, I went over to New Albany.

October

Wednesday, 1st. Left Jeffersonville for home. 2d. At home. Solemnized marriage between Mr. Fred Helwig and Miss Anna Kupfer. Conducted a service after the wedding. 3d and 4th. Quite busy at home. 5th. In Cincinnati. Conducted a service at St. Paul's Church; large congregation. Monday, 6th. Officiated at Dayton, Ohio, in the afternoon, baptizing the infant child of Mr. and Mrs. Hatfield. 7th. Reached home at 3 o'clock in the morning. Busy all day, and the next. 9th. Went to Detroit to attend the Church Congress; met many of the clergy, including

Dr. Gallaudet. Attending the sessions of the congress. Saturday, 11th. The Doctor and I reached Flint. Sunday, 14th. Flint. I officiated in the morning at the deaf-mute school, the Doctor preaching at St. Paul's Church. At 3 o'clock P. M. a Service for deaf-mutes only was held at the church; and at 7:30 P. M. a combined service; Rev. Mr. Seabrease, the Rector, assisted. 13th. East Saginaw. Guests of the Rev. Mr. Masker. Combined service at St. Paul's church in the evening. 14th. At Ann Arbor. Combined service in the Chapel of St. Andrew's Church. I baptized an infant daughter of deaf-mute parents. 15th. Ypsilanti. A similar service at St. Luke's Church, assisted by the Rector, the Rev. T. W. McLean. Dr. Gallaudet left at midnight for New York. 16th. I went to Marshall, Mich., and held a service for deaf-mutes only at 3 o'clock P. M. 17th. Combined service at Trinity Church, Niles, assisted by the Rector, the Rev. C. C. Tate. The mutes came long distances to attend this service, which is the case almost everywhere. 18th. In Chicago. Sunday, 19th. Attended a morning worship at St. James' Church. Conducted a service at 3 o'clock P. M., and left soon after for home. 20th. At home, tired and sleepy from the ride all night. 21st. Called on Bishop Bedell. Studying and attending to correspondence. 23rd. Service in the Chapel of Grace Church, Cleveland. The mutes saw for the first time their memorial of Rev. A. H. Washburn, D.D.—a beautiful brass altar desk. 24th. Busy all day. 25th. Went to Pittsburgh. Called on Mr. Thaw. Sunday, 26th. Conducted a service in the Chapel of Trinity Church at 3 o'clock P. M. 27th. At St. Paul's Church, Cleveland. Attended a celebration of the twenty-fifth anniversary of the consecration of Bishop Bedell. Among those present and making addresses, were Bishops Stevens, Jaggar and Whitehead; Rev. Drs. Burr, Bronson and Bodine; Ex-President Hayes and General Devereux. 28th. Present at the consecration of Rev. Dr. Rulison to the Assistant Episcopate of Central Pennsylvania. 29th. Attended a meeting of the Sunday School Institute, at Trinity Church, Cleveland. 30th and 31st. Busy preparing a lecture.

November

Saturday, 1st. Busy preparing for to-morrow. Sunday 2d. Officiated twice at Grace Church, Cleveland. 3d, 4th and 5th. Busy writing letters and arranging a new schedule of appointments. 6th and 7th. Busy with my annual report to go into the Appendix of the Report of the Eastern Society. 8th. Started in the morning for Indianapolis, expecting to lecture in the evening at the Institution. A wreck on the railroad delayed the train so that the appointment could not be met. Sunday, 9th. Indianapolis. Conducted two services at the Institution, and one at Christ Church. 10th. Went to Jeffersonville, Indiana, and conducted a service at St. Paul's Church, with a good congregation. 11th. Attended a convocation at New Albany in the forenoon. In the evening lectured at Gresham's Hall, Jeffersonville, on the life and writings of Washington Irving. Guest of Mr. E. W. Fitch. 13th. Reached home at 2 o'clock in the morning. Busy during the day. Held service in the evening. 14th. Busy. 15th. Went to Columbus, Ohio, and lectured in the evening at the Institution. Subject: "The Life and Writings of Washington Irving." Sunday, 16th. Conducted morning service at the Institution, and attended morning worship at Trinity Church. Conducted service at Trinity Church at 3 o'clock; and a combined service at half past 7 o'clock, with the assistance of the Rector, the Rev. C. H. Babcock. Left Columbus at midnight. 17th. Norwalk. Ohio, conducted service at 3 o'clock in the afternoon, and then returned home. 18th and 19th. Busy revising history. 20th. Helped one in distress. Lectured in the evening. 22d. In Chicago. Called on Bishop McLaren. Distributed annual reports. Lectured before the Pas a Pas Club of deaf-mutes, on life and writings of Irving. Sunday, 23d. Officiated for deaf-mutes, at three o'clock P. M. at St. James' Church. 24th. Reached home tired and sleepy from the ride all night. Did what I could during the day. 25th and 26th. Busy. 27th. Thanksgiving day. Conducted morning service at Grace Church, Cleveland. Self and family dined at Mrs. Washburn;s. Attended a gathering of deaf-mutes in the evening. 28th. Left in the afternoon for the East. 29th. Reached New York. Went directly to St.

Ann's Rectory. Met Dr. Gallaudet and family, also, Rev. Messrs. Chamberlain and Colt. Sunday, 30th. Morning, officiated at the Institution, at Fanwood. Afternoon, officiated at St. Ann's, with a large congregation. Addressed the Bible Class afterwards, in the basement. Evening, at the Church of the Messiah, Brooklyn, made a brief address on the Western work, which was interpreted orally by Dr. Gallaudet.

December

Monday, 1st. Called at the rooms of the Committee on Domestic Missions and met the Rev. G. F. Flichtner, the secretary, with whom I had a brief consultation; handed him my quarterly report. Called on Mr. J. D. Layng, an old Western friend, and on others. 2d. Called at the Home for Aged and Infirm Deaf-Mutes, and met Miss Middleton, the kind hearted matron. Wednesday, 3d. Went to Washington, D. C. Was a guest of President Gallaudet, of the National College for the Deaf, at Kendall Green. 4th. Conducted the morning service in the primary department, at 8:15 o'clock, and in the College Chapel at 9 o'clock. Visited several classes and recitation rooms. After dinner, President Gallaudet took me over the city in his carriage. I very greatly enjoyed the ride, which took me through the most interesting portions of this "city of magnificent distances." 5th. Took the Chapel service in the primary department. Spent the time from 9 A. M. till 4 P. M. in the city, visiting the Capitol, Smithsonian Institute, National Museum, Washington Monument, the White House, and other objects of national interest. 6th. Went to Baltimore. Mr. Wells, the faithful deaf-mute lay-reader, met me at the station, and took me to his house. Afternoon, we called together on the late Dr. Leeds. Sunday, 7th. Baltimore. Morning, combined service at Trinity Church, with the Rector, the Rev. Geo. A. Leakin. Afternoon, service for deaf-mutes only, in the Chapel of Grace Church, with a large congregation. Evening, combined service at Grace Church, Rev. George Leeds, D.D., Rector. His assistant, the Rev. Mr. Regester, read my address to the hearing portion of the congregation. 8th. Visited the colored school for deaf-mutes, on Saratoga street. Rev. Dr. Gallaudet arrived in Baltimore to-day. We had a brief and interesting consultation. Before leaving this city I met a Western friend, Mr. J. B. Washington, of Pittsburgh. Dr. Gallaudet left for New York, and I for Frederick, Md. 9th. Frederick. State School for Deaf-Mutes. Conducted the morning service in the Chapel, and soon after took the train for Romney, W. Va., which was reached at sundown. Mr. A. D. Hays met me at the station, and took me to their hotel. 10th. Romney. Visited the Institution with Mrs. Hays. Took tea with Prof. Chapin. 11th. Romney. Took the Chapel service at 7:45 A. M. Dined at the Institution, with Superintendent Covell. Took tea at Mr. Chidester's. 12th. Left Romney early. 13th. Reached home at 6 o'clock A. M. Found a good sized mail. Sunday, 14th. Officiated twice at Grace Church, Cleveland. 15th. Busy with correspondence and a new schedule of appointments. 16th, 17th, 18th, and 19th. At home at work every day. 20th. Went to Cincinnati. Sunday, 21st. Assisted the Rev. Dr. Benedict in the administration of Holy Communion. Afternoon, conducted a service for deaf-mutes at St. Paul's Church. 22d. Reached home early in the morning. 25th. Conducted Christmas service at Grace Church, Cleveland. 26th. Busy packing household effects. 27th. Went to Detroit. Sunday 28th. Officiated twice in the Chapel of St. John's Church; Rector, the Rev. George Worthington, S.T.D. Monday, 29th. Hastings, Mich. Combined service, assisted by the Rector, the Rev. J. W. Bancroft. 30th. Reached home greatly fatigued. Went to work at once with preparations to move. 31st. Moved to 82 Woodland Court, Cleveland, O.

January, 1885

Thursday, 1st. At our new home. 2d. Busy getting our household things in order. Saturday, 3d. Went to Wilkinsburg, Pa., then to Pittsburgh. Sunday, 4th. Morning, assisted the Rev. Samuel Maxwell in administering the Holy Communion, at Trinity Church. Afternoon, conducted the usual deaf-mute service. Evening, with the Rev. George Hodges, in a combined service at St. Stephen's Mission, Wilkinsburg, which is now the seat of the new Western Pennsylvania School for the Deaf. Met the Rev. Boyd Vincent at this service. 5th. Visited the school in question, and conducted the morning service in the Chapel. Returned to Pittsburgh and called on Mr. W. C. Quincy. Returned home in the evening. 6th. Busy in various ways. 7th and 8th. Busy getting things in order in our new home. Saturday, 10th. In Chicago. Made a short call on Bishop McLaren; made other calls. Felt slightly ill and retired early. Sunday, 11th. Morning, attended worship at St. James' Church. Dined with Dr. Vibbert. Afternoon, deaf-mute service, and baptism of infant daughter of Mr. and Mrs. Christenson. 12th. Chicago. Made several calls. Left in the evening 13th. Reached home after traveling all night, much fatigued. Answered a number of letters. 14th, 15th and 16th. Variously occupied. Saturday, 17th. Very cold day. Left for St. Louis. Sunday, 18th. Train four hours late, so that I missed the morning service at Christ Church. Afternoon, conducted the usual deaf-mute service. Monday, 19th. Called on Bishop Robertson and others. Afternoon, visited the day school for deaf-mutes, and told the pupils some stories. Evening, lectured before the deaf-mute society. 20th. Stopped at Terre Haute two hours on my way from St. Louis. Reaching Indianapolis in the evening, I found that the Bishop was out of town. Took tea with Rev. Dr. Jenckes. Reached home early in the morning of the 21st. On this day, and the following, I acknowledged a number of letters, and worked on a new schedule of appointments. 23d and 24th. Engaged in study. Sunday, 25th. Two services—morning and afternoon—at Grace Church, Cleveland. At the last service two adult deaf-mutes received the sacrament of baptism. Monday, 26th. Attended the funeral of the Rev. J. W. Clark, at St. James' Church. 27th. Busy in doors all day. 28th. Went to Pittsburgh. 29th. Returned home. 31st. Indianapolis. Dined with the Bishop, and had a consultation. Called on Rev. Dr. Bradley. Lectured at the Institution in the evening.

February

Sunday, 1st. Morning, conducted service at the Indiana Institution, at 9 o'clock and hastened to morning service at Christ Church. Assisted in the administration of the Holy Communion. Afternoon, service at 2:30 o'clock at the Institution, and at 4 o'clock at Christ Church. Monday, 2d. Reached home in the morning. Very cold day. Went out on business. 3d. Called at the office of *The Standard of the Cross.* 4th and 5th. In doors engaged variously. Wrote acknowledgements to Bishop Gillespie and Mr. W. R. Shelby. Wrote Bishop Welles and Mr. Layng. Received a check from Rev. Dr. Worthington. 6th. Went to Gambier to see Bishop Bedell. Arrived at noon, and held a consultation with him at "Kokosing." Met Dr. Bodine, president of Kenyon College; took tea with him. Reached Columbus at night. 7th. Dayton, Ohio. Lectured on Washington Irving. Sunday, 8th. Dayton. Morning, Holy Communion at 8:30, the deaf-mute communicants received with the others. Deaf-mute service at 10:30 o'clock, in the Ladies' Room of Christ Church. Afternoon, service in the Church, with baptism of two infant children of deaf-mute parents. Monday, 9th. Reached home. Busy on this and the two following days. 12th. A daughter was born to us. 14th, 15th, 16th and 17th. Variously engaged at home. 18th. Ash Wednesday. Conducted a service at Grace Church, with a large congregation. 19th. Contributed as usual to the postal revenue of the government. Made several calls. 20th. Left home. 21st. In Chicago, making calls. Attended a deaf-mute social in the evening. Sunday, 22d. Morning, attended worship at St. James' Church, and afterwards dined with Dr. Vibbert. Afternoon, conducted service, with a good sized congregation. At 5 o'clock I baptized an infant child of deaf-mutes, at their house. Monday, 23d. At Columbus, Ohio, making several calls. Baptized a deaf-mute woman at a house. Dined at the Institution. Reached home at midnight. 24th and 25th. Time divided between reading and writing. 26th. Began to arrange a schedule of appointments for myself and Rev. Dr. Gallaudet. Held a service in the evening at Grace Church. 28th. Went to Detroit. Made several calls.

March

Sunday, 1st. Detroit. Morning service and Holy Communion at St. John's Church. Evening service at the same place. 2d. Returned home, and found a check for $50 from Helen A. DeKoven, of Chicago. 3d. Went to Columbus and solemnized marriage between Mr. Charles Henry Green and Miss Annie Eliza Theiss, at Trinity Church. Left at midnight. 4th. At Grace Church, Mansfield, Ohio, conducting a service in the evening. 5th. At three o'clock in the morning I reached home. During the day a large mail occupied my attention. 6th. Mailed a number of letters, and planned a new schedule of appointments. Sunday, 8th. Christ Church, St. Louis. Afternoon, conducted a service with a large congregation. Attended evening service at St. George's Church. Monday, 9th. Visited the day school for deaf-mutes, and told the pupils some stories. Left St. Louis in the evening, and reached home next afternoon very much fatigued. 11th. Busy at home all day. 12th. Conducted a service at Grace Church, Cleveland. Met my catechumens afterwards. 13th. Went to Pittsburgh, and made several business calls. Sunday, 15th. Trinity Church. Morning, baptized an adult deaf-mute, who, with his brother-in-law, also a mute, was soon afterwards confirmed by Bishop Whitehead. I interpreted. They soon after received their first Communion. Afternoon. conducted the usual service at Trinity Church. Guest of Mr. McClurg. Monday, 16th. Combined service at St. Stephen's Church, McKeesport, Pa., with the assistance of the Rector, the Rev. H. Greenfield Schorr. 17th. Reached home in the evening. 18th. Close to my desk all day, and most of the next. 19th. Took a service at Grace Church, Cleveland; good congregation, despite the extreme cold. 20th In Columbus, Ohio. Guest of Mr. Robert Patterson. Saturday, 21st. making calls. In the afternoon I instructed several candidates for baptism. Sunday, 22d. Morning, officiated at the Institution at 9:45 o'clock, and hastened to morning service at Trinity Church. Afternoon, 3 o'clock, conducted service at Church, baptizing seventeen persons and addressing them. Took tea at Mr. McGregor's. 23rd. Portsmouth, Ohio. Combined

service at All Saints' Church, assisted by the Rector, the
Rev. H. L. Badger, and the Rev. Mr. Maguire, of Christ
Church. Many were present, including a good number of
deaf-mutes. 24th. In Columbus. Addressed a Society at the
Institution in the evening. 25th. Afternoon, met my
catechumens and instructed them. In the evening, Bishop
Penick confirmed a class of twenty-four deaf-mutes, the
largest that I have ever presented. Left for home at
midnight 26th. Busy all day at home. Received a check
from Mr. White, Treasurer of the Diocese of Pittsburgh.
27th. Mailed forty letters and postals. Went down town on
business. Sunday, 29th. Chicago. Morning, Bishop
McLaren confirmed a large class at St. James' Church, two
being deaf-mutes. Afternoon, conducted the usual silent
service, and left immediately for Michigan City. Monday,
30th. At the hospitable home of the Rev. E. S. Burford,
Rector of St. Mark's Church, Grand Rapids, Mich. Held a
service, and administered baptism in the evening. 31st.
At Kalamazoo. Service in a room of the parish house.
Guest of the Rev. R. E. Jones.

April

Wednesday, 1st. Called up at midnight, after resting but
two hours. Reached home late in the following night. 2d.
and 3d. Assisted a deaf-mute in distress. 4th. Left home
in the evening. Sunday, 5th. Indianapolis. Morning,
officiated at the Institution, and then went to Christ
Church. Afternoon, took another service at the
Institution at 2:30 o'clock, and hastened to Christ Church
to officiate at 5 o'clock. Good congregation. Bishop
Knickerbacker was present. Evening, combined service at
Christ Church. The Bishop confirmed three deaf-mutes in
a class presented by the Rev. E. A Bradley. Monday, 6th.
Left Indianapolis at four o'clock in the morning. Held two
services at St. Paul's Church, Kenton, Ohio. Baptized three
adults. Rev. George Bosley assisted at the combined
service. Left Kenton at night. 7th. Reached home in the
afternoon. 8th, 9th, and 10th. Quite busy arranging a new
schedule of appointments, and writing the notices to
individuals and the press. 11th. Went to Detroit. Sunday,
12th. Officiated in the Chapel of St. John's Church,

Detroit, in the evening. Monday, 13th. Assisted by the Rev J. E. Walton, held a combined service at Trinity Church, Marshall, Mich. 14th. Held a service at Jackson, Mich. 15th. Held a service at St. Paul's Church, Flint, and left at night. 16th. Reached home in the afternoon. 17th and 18th. Mailed reports and vouchers; wrote Bishop Seymour. Sunday, 19th. Officiated twice in the Chapel of Grace Church, Cleveland. 20th, 21st, 22d, 23d and 24th. Re-writing an address, besides doing other work. Received a package of 300 reports from Rev. Dr. Gallaudet. Sunday, 26th. Held a service at 3 o'clock at Christ Church, St. Louis. At its close I went to Alton, Ill., and held a service at the Rectory. 27th. Rev. Messrs. Whitmarsh and Hefter assisted me at a combined service at St. Paul's Church, Carlinsville, Ill. 28th. At the Deanery, Carrollton. Dean Whitmarsh and I conducted a combined service at Trinity Church. 29th. Jacksonville. Seat of the Illinois School for the Deaf. Conducted service at Trinity Church, Rector, the Rev. Dr. Easter. 30th. Combined service at Christ Church, Ottawa, Ill., assisted by the Rev. N. W. Hermans, the Rector.

May

Friday, 1st. Held a service for deaf-mutes at Christ Church, Joliet. 2d. Went to Milwaukee, and returned to Chicago in the evening. Sunday, 3d. Service in the afternoon, at St. James' Church. 4th. Reached home from Chicago. Close to my desk all day, as well as the 5th, 6th, and 7th: Called on Bishop Bedell and had an interesting consultation. 8th. Preparing a sermon for Cincinnati. Sunday, 10th. Deaf-mute service at St. Paul's Church, Cincinnati. Went to Dayton and held service in the evening at Christ Church. Monday, 11th. Combined service at Grace Church, Galion, Ohio, assisted by the Rev. W. M. Brown, the Rector. Large congregation. 12th. Busy at home. 28th. Mailed annual reports to Bishops Gillespie, Welles, and Whipple. Solemnized marriage in the evening between Mr. Gustave Hank and Miss Margaret B. Schaefer. 14th. Getting ready to go to New York, for which place I left on the following day. Saturday, 16th. New York. Went to No. 9 West 18th Street. Called to see the

Rev. Mr. Flichtner, at the Bible House, but he was out of town. Went to the book store of Mr. Pott, and purchased tracts. Mr. Pott, as treasurer of the Prayer Book Society, made the Western Deaf-Mute Mission another donation of fifty Prayer Books.   Dined with the Rev. John Chamberlain, at 1151 Broadway. Sunday, 17th. Morning. Preached for the Rev. Anson T. Colt, in the chapel of Grace Church, Jersey City. Afternoon. Took the service at St. Ann's Church for deaf-mutes, in West 18th Street, near Fifth Avenue. Evening. Preached again for the Rev. Mr. Colt in the Chapel of St. Ann's Church, Brooklyn. Monday, 18th. Called on Mr. J. D. Layng; and made a few purchases at the Church book store.   Tuesday 19th. Newburgh, N. Y. Visited Washington's Headquarters. Held a combined service at St. George's Church in the evening, assisted by the Rev. Dr. Applegate. 20th. At Poughkeepsie. Guest of Mrs. C. M. Nelson. Visited Vassar College in her company.   Combined services in the evening, at Christ Church. 21st. Reached Buffalo at midnight, and went to a hotel. 22d. Reached home in the afternoon. 23d. Busy till night when I took the sleeping car for Pittsburgh. Sunday, 24th.   Reached Calvary Church, East End, in time for morning service: after which I went to the Western Pennsylvania School for the Deaf, located at Edgewood, and conducted service.   At 4:30 P. M., I held another service at St. Stephen's Church, Wilkinsburg.   25th. Reached home in the evening.   26th and 27th.   Busy arranging a schedule of appointments for self and and the Rev. Mr. Chamberlain. Called on Bishop Bedell and Gen. Devereux. 28th and 29th. Close to my desk. 30th. Dr. Gallaudet arrived from New York. Sunday, 31st. Morning. Grace Church, Cleveland.   Dr. Gallaudet baptized our infant daughter, and preached for the Rector, the Rev. F. M. Clendenin. I preached to the deaf-mutes at the same time.   Afternoon.   The Doctor and myself conducted a silent service for deaf-mutes only, at 3 o'clock. Evening. Combined service at Grace Church.

June

Monday, 1st.   Combined service at St. Paul's Church, Norwalk, assisted by Dr. Gallaudet and the Rector, Rev.

Mr. Aves. We also held a service in the afternoon for deaf-mutes only. Tuesday, 2d. Grace Church, Mansfield, Ohio. Deaf-mute service at 3 o'clock, and a combined service in the evening, with baptism of three persons. 3d. At the Ohio Institution for the Education of Deaf-Mutes, Columbus; visited several classes. Combined service at Trinity Church in the evening, assisted by the Rev. C. H. Babcock. 4th. Dr. Gallaudet and myself conducted service in the Institution Chapel, and then left for Urbana, O. Before the combined service at the Church of the Epiphany, we enjoyed a carriage ride with the Rev. E. H. McGuffey, the Rector. Friday, 5th. At Indianapolis. Called at the Institution, after consulting with the Rev. Dr. Bradley, with whom we afterwards took tea. Combined service at Christ Church in the evening. Saturday, 6th. At a reunion of deaf-mutes held at Newcastle, Ind. Sunday, 7th. Morning, combined service at the Fair Ground, Newcastle, Dr. Gallaudet preaching orally, and myself by signs, simultaneously. Afternoon, another combined service, the Doctor reading my sermon orally; about 4,000 people at the last service. At 5 o'clock P. M., I married Mr. Amos Wrights and Miss Emma Coppock; and baptized them shortly afterwards. Evening, combined service at the Christian Meeting House, which was full to its utmost capacity. Monday, 8th. Richmond, Ind. We dined at the house of R. H. Shoemaker, where we met several persons, among them, Rev. Frank Hallam and Mrs. O. P. Morton. After dinner we had a pleasant drive out on the National Road with our host. Before tea at the house of Mrs. Craighead, we called on Mrs. J. S. Brown and her daughter. The combined service in the evening was held with the assistance of the Rev. Mr. Hallam. Tuesday, 9th. On our way to Cincinnati we stopped for an hour at Dayton, and made a short call on the Rev. Mr. Webster. Combined service in the evening at St. Paul's Church, Cincinnati, Rev. Dr. Benedict assisting. Wednesday, 10th. At the above named church, at 4 o'clock P. M., assisted by Dr. Gallaudet, I solemnized marriage between Mr. Henry Cheney White, B. A., and Miss Mary Elizabeth Mann. Soon afterwards we dined with the couple and a few friends, at the St. Nicholas. The couple left for their far western home soon afterwards. Mr. White has charge of the Utah School for Deaf-Mutes, located at Salt Lake City. 11th. Reaching home with the Doctor, I found a good sized mail.   We attended the Diocesan Convention, held at St. John's Church, Cleveland, meeting the Bishop and many of the clergy. 12th. Dr. Gallaudet left for the East in the morning.   13th.   Very busy all day.   Sunday, 14th. Officiated twice in the Chapel of Grace Church, Cleveland. 15th.   Received check from Rev. G. F. Flichtner.   Mailed items to the Church papers. 16th, 17th and 18th. Engaged in preparations for the Northwestern trip. Friday, 19th. In company with the Rev. John Chamberlain, I left home. At Chicago we conducted a service for deaf-mutes. Saturday, 20th. We went to Milwaukee, and called at the Clergy House, where we met the Rev. C. L. Mallory, Dean of the Cathedral. In the evening we reached Delevan, Wis., the seat of the State School for the Deaf, where we remained during the reunion of the Alumni. Sunday, 21st. Attended morning worship at Christ Church, Rev. Charles Holmes, Rector. At 3 o'clock P. M., we conducted a sign service at the Institution. At 7:30 P. M. we had a combined service at the Church. I baptized two adults and an infant. Monday, 22d. Attending the reunion a part of the day. Reached Milwaukee in the evening. Rev. Mr. Chamberlain remained at Develan. In Milwaukee I had an interesting consultation with Bishop Welles. 23d. After a short stay in Minneapolis, I left for Faribault, Minn., which I reached at sundown; went to the State School for the Deaf, where I had a cordial reception at the hands of the Superintendent. Wednesday, 24th. Called on Bishop Whipple; also on the Rev. A. A. Abbott, Dean of the Cathedral of our Merciful Saviour. Thursday, 25th. Opened the session of the Minnesota Deaf-Mute Alumni Association with prayer. Made a few short addresses. In the evening I conducted a service in the room where the session was held. Rev. Mr. Abbott called in the forenoon. Friday, 26th. The delegates went away on an excursion to one of the lakes near Faribault. I remained at the Institute for rest and study. In the evening, attended a reception tendered by the Principal and his wife. Saturday, 27th. After reaching Minneapolis and consulting with Rev. Dr.

Wells, I went out with Rev. Mr. Hixon to the summer cabin of Rev. A. R. Graves, in the woods three miles away. Sunday, 28th. Morning combined service at Gethsemane Church, Minneapolis, assisted by the Rev. Mr. Hixon. Church full. Afternoon silent service at the same Church. Evening, service at St. Mark's Church. The Rev. T. B. Wells read the evening service and my written sermon, while I interpreted for deaf-mutes. Remained over night at the rectory. Monday, 29th. After spending the rest of the forenoon at St. Paul, I left for Wisconsin. 30th. After resting at Camp Douglass, I reached Oshkosh in the afternoon. There I met the Rev. Mr. Chamberlain. Assisted by the Rev. Mr. Greenwood, we held a combined service in the evening at Trinity Church, with a good sized congregation. We were the guests of Mr. Hutchinson.

With this, closes the Tenth Annual Report of Church Work among Deaf-Mutes in the Central Western and North Western Dioceses. The retrospect of the year, as well as of the nine years preceding, is full of encouragement, as the following summarized statement shows:

SUMMARY

Services held during the year	170
Baptisms	56
Confirmations	48
Marriages	7
Candidates awaiting confirmation	16
Total services in ten years	1400
Total baptisms	297
Present number of communicants	249
Total marriages	35
Total Parishes served	192

FROM LAST YEAR'S REPORT

Services during the year	148
Baptisms	32
Confirmations	29
Marriages	3
Total Parishes service	168

ACKNOWLEDGEMENTS

The thanks of the Church are due, and they are hereby tendered, the officers of the railway lines who have recognized the exceptional character of the Mission, and rendered the pursuit of its work over a vast area possible. Deaf-mutes are few and widely scattered, rendering much travel necessary on the part of their minister in spiritual things. Being thus few, and of moderate means, they cannot meet his traveling expenses.

The New York, and the Bishop White Prayer Book Societies through their Secretaries, Messrs. Pott and Biddle, have again favored the Western Deaf-Mute Mission with Prayer Books and Hymnals. These have been judiciously distributed.

My thanks are due *The Churchman, Living Church, Standard of the Cross, Church Press, The Church, Church News, Southern Ohio Church Chronicle, Church Helper, Church Worker,* and *Iowa Churchman,* for publishing Ephphatha appeals and acknowledgments without charge. Thanks are also tendered the daily and weekly papers of many places for the free publication of notices of services.

The valuable assistance rendered by the brethren of the clergy is greatly appreciated. They have reached the deaf-mutes living within their parochial limits with notices of special services, and encouraged their attendance at the regular services, by inducing their people to show them the places in the Prayer Book.

During my visits to St. Louis I have been hospitably entertained at St. Luke's Hospital, under the charge of the Sisterhood of the Good Shepherd. For ten years I have enjoyed their hospitality.

I must not omit to thank the *Deaf-Mutes' journal, Deaf-Mute Advance, Deaf-Mute Mirror, The Vis-a-Vis, Deaf-Mute Record, Deaf-Mute Companion, Nebraska Journal, Kentucky Deaf-Mute,* and *Kansas Star,* for kindly publishing my appointments.

SECTION B.

JOHN CARLIN

A layman—a deaf man of unusual talents—who gave much support in many ways to the ministry of the Rev. Thomas Gallaudet and gave inspiration to the deaf community in this country, was Mr. John Carlin,[*] born deaf in Philadelphia in 1813. He graduated from the Pennsylvania School for the Deaf in that city in 1825. Mention of Mr. Carlin has already been made in this book.

Mr. Carlin was present at the March 3rd, 1853, meeting held in the small chapel of New York University and he spoke in favor of a motion to obtain for St. Ann's Church for the Deaf a building and so make it a parish with T.Gallaudet as rector, within the Diocese of New York. Under his leadership a group of deaf people raised $6,000 for the building fund.

It was Mr. Carlin who suggested a monument to the memory of Thomas Hopkins Gallaudet (father of T.Gallaudet), and he influenced Edward Miner Gallaudet (a brother of T.Gallaudet) to found a college for the deaf. At the formal opening of Gallaudet College (now University) in 1864 Mr. Carlin made the oration. The first degree of Master of Arts conferred by the college was awarded this man.

When a convention was held in 1881 at Harrisburg, Pa., and the Pennsylvania Society for the Deaf came into being Mr. Carlin served as president *pro tem* until the election, when the Rev. Henry W. Syle of Philadelphia was named president of the new organization. At that time Mr. Carlin was a trustee of the Church Mission to Deaf-Mutes; T.Gallaudet was director.

---

[*] Bibliography: *The Frat*, publication of the National Fraternal Society of the Deaf.

John Carlin

A biographer has said of him—

> After studying drawing and portrait painting, he went to London in 1838 and made studies from the antiques in the British Museum.   Later, he studied more art in Paris. Returning to America in 1841, he settled down in New York City as a painter of miniatures.
>
> About the same time he blossomed out as a poet and author, publishing some verses and a series of articles in the Philadelphia Saturday Courier.   His achievement was astonishing....
>
> In 1873 he headed the committee to raise a building fund for the Gallaudet Home for Aged and Infirm Deaf in Wappinger Falls, N.Y., and served until 1881.   He married Miss Seward of the family of Lincoln's Secretary Seward.

On April 23, 1891, this great artist, poet and advocate, who did so much on behalf of the deaf community, departed this life at the age of 78.

SECTION C.

Thomas Gallaudet Plants Seed in Philadelphia

A history of All Soul's Church for the Deaf, Philadelphia, published by the Pennsylvania Diocesan Commission on Church Work Among the Deaf during the episcopate of the Rt. Rev. Bishop O. W. Whitaker and the pastorate of the Rev. Charles O. Dantzer.

The Church's mission to the "Children of Silence" in the city of Philadelphia had its beginning in a service held in St. Stephen's Church, Rev. Dr. Duchachet then being rector, on the evening of Friday, March 4, 1859, by the Rev. Dr. Thomas Gallaudet of sainted memory. Dr. Gallaudet had his own growing work in New York City to attend to, but he arranged to visit Philadelphia quarterly for services in the sign-language.   These services were continued until 1861, when the Mission to the Deaf became identified with an effort to organize a new parish to be called St. John Chrysostom, under the Rev. Dr. Samuel Cox. The service was held in the chapel of the Episcopal Academy, the idea evidently being to build up a parish for the hearing and deaf jointly, like St. Ann's in New York of that day.   This effort, it seems, did not succeed, but not until a building fund amounting to $2,000 had been raised, partly by the hearing congregation and partly by the deaf.

On December 19, 1864, Bishop Alonzo Potter presided at a meeting called to devise means of resuming and continuing the services for the deaf. Dr. Gallaudet made the principal address, and on motion of Bishop Stevens (the Assistant Bishop) a committee was appointed to further the work. Shortly after this the Rev. Dillon Eagan, who was Dr. Gallaudet's assistant at St. Ann's Church, New York, was called to the rectorship of Calvary Monumental Church at Front and Margaretta Streets.

The formal union of the Mission to the Deaf with this parish was effected on Sunday, October 8, 1865, Bishop Stevens preaching the sermon.   The building fund of $2,000 mentioned above was turned over to the vestry and expended in various improvements to the church and a deaf man was chosen to the vestry. In 1866, Mr. Eagan left the parish, and the Rev. Dr. Francis J. Clerc, a son of Laurent Clerc, the first deaf teacher of the deaf in America, was called to Calvary. Dr. Clerc was a past master of the sign-language, it being the language with which he was familiar from childhood, from constant use in his intercourse with his deaf parents, and his labors among the deaf were productive of much good. But in 1868 he became warden of Burd Orphan Asylum of St. Stephen's Church, stipulating, however, that he could be free to give Sunday afternoons to the Mission at Calvary.   This church proving unsuitable for it, with the permission of the Rev. Dr. Rudder, the Sunday School Room of St. Stephen's Church was used.   Without any formal severance of relations with Calvary Church, the Mission simply followed Dr. Clerc to St. Stephen's.   In March, 1870, the question was agitated of buying a small church on Ninth Street, near Buttonwood, for a chapel of St. Stephen's and for the use of the Mission, but nothing came of it, and the deaf continued to use St. Stephen's Sunday School. On March 2, 1872, Dr. Rudder in the presence of wardens, vestry and congregation formally accepted the Mission as a part of the parish. In May, 1872, Dr. Clerc was called to Burlington College, N.J., and thereafter the supply of services devolved upon Dr. Gallaudet, with a quarterly service by Dr. Clerc.   Shortly after this a remarkable deaf man, Henry Winter Syle, appeared; he was destined to build up a more enduring work among the deaf of Philadelphia.--Reprinted from "A Missionary Chronicle."

BIBLIOGRAPHY

CHAPTERS 1 & 2

Boatner, Maxine Tull. *Voice of the Deaf;* a biography of Edward Miner Gallaudet. Public Affairs Press, Washington, D.C., c1959. 190p.

Gallaudet, (Rev'd) Thomas. *A Letter to Aunt Mary,* dated March 19, 1844. From private collection. Gallaudet U. Archives.

Gallaudet, (Rev'd) Thomas. *A Sketch of My Life.* Unpublished. Ms., Gallaudet U. Archives

Gallaudet, Edward M. *Life of Thomas Hopkins Gallaudet,* Founder of Deaf–Mute Instruction in America. Henry Holt & Co., New York, 1888. 339p.

Gallaudet, Thomas Hopkins. *Discourses on various points of Christian Faith and practice::* most of which were delivered in the Chapel of the Oratoire in Paris in the spring of 1816. Published in 1818. Gallaudet University Archives.

Humphrey, (Rev'd) Hemen. *The Life and Labors of the Rev. T. H. Gallaudet, LL.D.* Robert Carter & Brothers, New York, 1857.

CHAPTER 3

An Interesting Ceremony (Gallaudet-Budd wedding). Printed in the New York Commercial Advertiser, July 16, 1845.

Currier, Enoch Henry. *Institutional Education and the Efficiency of Rev. Dr. Thomas Gallaudet as a Teacher and Director.* Eighty-fourth Annual Report and Documents, 1903, New York Institution for the Instruction of the Deaf & Dumb. (pp. 121-131).

Gallaudet, (Rev'd) Thomas. *A Letter to the President of the New England Gallaudet Association.* Printed in The American Annals of the Deaf (AAD), Vol. 9:186-7 (1857).

Gallaudet, (Rev'd) Thomas. *An Incident in Laura Bridgeman's Early Life.* Printed in the Deaf-Mutes' Journal (DMJ), June 13, 1889.

Gallaudet, (Rev'd) Thomas. *Reminiscences of H. P. Peet.* AAD 18:103-5 (1873).

Gallaudet, (Rev'd) Thomas. *School Room Arrangements.* AAD 3:74-6 (1850).

Gallaudet, (Rev'd) Thomas. *The Mental State of the Uneducated.* AAD 6:136 (1854).

Hotspur. *Some Reminiscences of the 50th Street Institution, its Inmates and Surroundings.* Printed in the DMJ, June 15, 1885.

New York Institution for the Instruction of the Deaf & Dumb. The Annual Report and Documents, 25th-40th (1844-1859) and 48th-84th (1866-1902).

New York Institution. AAD 25:288 (1880).

CHAPTER 4

Berg, (Rev'd) Otto B. *A Missionary Chronicle;* being a history of the ministry to the deaf in the Episcopal Church (1850-1980). Published by Episcopal Conference of the Deaf, 1984. 272p.

Braddock, (Rev'd) Guilbert C. *Notable Deaf Persons—No. 49: Cornelia A. Lathrop.* Printed in THE FRAT, January 1941.

Braddock, (Rev'd) Guilbert C. Report on St. Ann's Church for the Deaf. Unpublished ms.

Braddock, (Rev'd) Guilbert C. *The Gallaudet Home.* DMJ, June 25, 1936.

Carlin, John. *The National Home for Aged and Infirm Deaf-Mutes.* The New York Times, September 1, 1875. Also Third Annual Report of Church Mission to Deaf-Mutes (1875).

Gallaudet, (Rev'd) Thomas. *A Record of the Marriages, Baptisms & Funeral Services Performed by Me.* Unpublished ms.

Gallaudet, (Rev'd) Thomas. *An Appeal.* The New York Times, February 9, 1899.

Gallaudet, (Rev'd) Thomas. *Church Work Among Deaf-Mutes, Past, Present and Future,* an address given at first meeting of the Conference of Church Workers Among the Deaf at St. Ann's Church for the Deaf, New York, 1881. Published in Proceedings.

Gallaudet, (Rev'd) Thomas. *Diary.* Unpublished ms.

Gallaudet, (Rev'd) Thomas. *Laying the Conerstone of St. Ann's Church.* The Churchman 78:269 (August 20, 1898); The Silent Worker, November 1898.

Gallaudet, (Rev'd) Thomas. *Parochial Register* of St. Ann's Church for the Deaf, New York City (1850-1868). Four volumes.

Gallaudet, (Rev'd) Thomas. *Parochial Reports* 1854-1901). Published in the Journal of the Proceedings of the Convention of the Protestant Episcopal Church in the Diocese of New York, 1854-1902.

Gallaudet, (Rev'd) Thomas. *Religious Services for Educated Deaf-Mutes.* AAD 5:124-6 (1853).

Gallaudet, (Rev'd) Thomas. *Sermon* preached at the 25th Anniversary of St. Ann's Church for Deaf-Mutes, 18th St. near Fifth Ave., N.Y., on the 19th Sunday after Trinity, October 7, 1877. AAD 23:131-2 (1878).

Gallaudet, (Rev'd) Thomas. *St. Ann's Church for Deaf-Mutes, New York.* (various titles of articles). AAD 5:128, 169-181 (1853); 8:172-85 (1856); 10:29-40, 163-76 (1858); 11:8-12, 207-10 (1859); 12:243-8 (1860); 13:191-2 (1868); 21:67 (1876); 25:98-9 (1880); 35:173-4 (1893); 38:173 (1893); 42:63 (1897); 43:138-9 (1898); 44:110-3 (1899); 45:165-6 (1900).

Gallaudet, (Rev'd) Thomas. *Statement on the 27th Anniversary of St. Ann's Church.* DMJ December 28, 1899.

Gallaudet, (Rev'd) Thomas. *The Church Mission to Deaf-Mutes.* Annual Reports, 1st-30th. (1873-1903). Also AAD 19:20 (1874).

Gallaudet, (Rev'd) Thomas. *The Twelfth Sunday After Trinity* (poem). AAD 24:261-2 (1879).

Whiting, (Rev'd) Eric J. *A Brief History of St. Ann's Church for the Deaf and Its Founder, the Rev. Dr. Thomas Gallaudet.* Unpublished ms.

CHAPTERS 5, 6, & 7

All Angels' Mission to the Deaf, Baltimore, Md. Sermon given on 40th anniversary by the Rev. Arthur C. Powell March 3d, 1899, at Grace Church. *Silent Worker,* March 1899.

All Souls' Church for the Deaf, Philadelphia, PA. *Our Fiftieth Year, 1888-1938.* Philadelphia, 1938. Unpub. ms.

Braddock, (Rev'd) Guilbert C. *Notable Deaf Persons—No. 64: Jonathan P. Marsh.* Printed in THE FRAT, April 1942.

Central New York Institution for Deaf-Mutes, Rome. *Annual Reports,* 1st-11th (1875-1885). Rome, N.Y.

Columbia Institution for the Deaf & Dumb, Washington, D.C. *Minutes of the Meeting of the Board of Directors, May 2, 1900.*

Conference of Principals of American Institutions for the Deaf, 4th (1880). Clarke Institution. *The Proceedings.* AAD 25:169-223 (1880).

Convention of American Instructors of the Deaf. *Proceedings* (7th-15th meetings). 1870-1898.

Dr. Gallaudet's First Visit to Chicago. Printed in the Bulletin & Quarterly Review, St. Ann's Church for the Deaf, v. 2, no. 1, July 1938.

Gallaudet, (Rev'd) Thomas. Address given at Inauguration of the College for the Deaf & Dumb at Washington, District of Columbia, June 28, 1864. pp. 61-2.

Gallaudet, (Rev'd) Thomas. *Deaf-Mute Associations.* AAD 9:186-7 (1856).

Gallaudet, (Rev'd) Thomas. *The Language of Motion;* a speech delivered at 2d convention of the Conference of Church Workers Among the Deaf in Philadelphia, Oct. 13-15, 1883. Published in 11th Annual Report (1883) of the Church Mission to Deaf-Mutes.

Joint Commission of Advice appointed by the General Convention, the Diocese of Virginia, Richmond. The Church Missions to the Deaf and Dumb. 1907. 4p.

Marsh, Jonathan P. *The Deaf-Mutes' Bible Class in Boston.* AAD 9:242-5 (1857).

Mission to Deaf-Mutes, Albany, N.Y. Pub. in 7th-12th Annual Reports (1879-1884) of the Church Mission to Deaf-Mutes. New York, 1879-1885.

Mission to the Deaf, Central New York and Western New York. Pub. in 10th Annual Report (1882) of The Church Mission to Deaf-Mutes, New York, 1882.

National Association of the Deaf. *Proceedings* of 1st convention held in Cincinnati, Ohio, in 1880. Pub. in DMJ, September 2, 1880.

New England Industrial School for the Education and Instruction of the Deaf-Mutes, Beverly, MA. *Annual Reports*, 1st-7th. Beverly, MA. 1881-1887.

Northern New York Institution for Deaf-Mutes at Malone. *Annual Reports*, 1st-12th. Malone, 1885-1896.

Patterson, Robert. *Semi-Centennial Celebration of the Ohio Institution.* AAD 24:252-60 (1874).

The Michigan Institution. AAD 17:59 (1872).

The Mid-Western Deaf-Mute Mission. Pub. in The Spirit of Missions 61:380-1 (August 1896).

Turner, (Rev'd) Job. *Report of the Mission to Deaf-Mutes in New England,* May 9, 1877 to October 31, 1877. Fifth Annual Report. The Church Mission to Deaf-Mutes, 1877. New York.

Williams, Lynne D. *The Rochester School for the Deaf, centennial history,* 1876-1976, Rochester, 1976.

CHAPTER 8

Gallaudet, (Rev'd) Thomas. A Journey to Europe, 1897. The 25th Annual Report of the Church Mission to Deaf-Mutes for the year ending Sept. 30, 1897.

Gallaudet, (Rev'd) Thomas. *A Letter to Elizabeth* (his daughter). dated Aug. 18, 1900, while in Paris. From private collection.

Gallaudet, (Rev'd) Thomas. *A Letter to the Editor.* DMJ, Aug. 29, 1901.

Gallaudet, (Rev'd) Thomas. *A Visit to Europe, 1889.* AAD 34:286-9 (1889).

Gallaudet, (Rev'd) Thomas. *An Expression of Thanks.* DMJ, April 1, 1889.

Gallaudet, (Rev'd) Thomas. *Dr. Gallaudet's European Trip.* DMJ, Aug. 16, 1888.

Gallaudet, (Rev'd) Thomas. *Home for the Aged and Infirm Deaf-Mutes.* Paper read at the Glasgow Deaf and Dumb Congress. In THE DEAF AND DUMB TIMES, v. 3, no. 5—Oct. 1891, pp.50-5.

Gallaudet, (Rev'd) Thomas. *Mission to the Adult Deaf and Dumb.* Paper read at the Glasgow Deaf and Dumb Congress. In THE DEAF AND DUMB TIMES, v.3, no. 5—Oct. 1891.

History of Our Deaf and Dumb Societies; the Missions to the Adult Deaf and Dumb of Ireland. THE BRITISH DEAF-MUTE AND DEAF CHRONICLE, v. 11, no. 15—Jan 1893.

Return From Europe. THE NEW YORK TIMES, Oct. 28, 1895.

Royal Association in Aid of the Deaf and Dumb. THE DEAF AND DUMB TIMES, v. 1, no. 2 (July 1889); v. 1; no. 3 (Aug. 1889); v. 1, no. 4 (Sept. 1889).

CHAPTER 9

A Golden Wedding (of Rev'd and Mrs. Thomas Gallaudet). AAD 40:312-5 (1895); DMJ, June 18, 1895; GALLAUDET ALUMNI BULLETIN, v. 3, no.9 (1948).

Rev. Dr. Gallaudet Receives the Homage of the Deaf on his Eightieth Birthday. DMJ, June 5, 1902.

Rev. Thomas Gallaudet: Fifty Years a Clergyman. THE NEW YORK TIMES, June 16, 1901.

The Rev. Thomas Gallaudet, D.D., L,H.D.—Fiftieth Anniversary of Your Ordination to the Priesthood. A document printed by St. Matterw's Parish in Manhattan, New York City.

CHAPTER 11

Tributes, eulogies and memorials to the Rev. Dr. Thomas Gallaudet that appeared in the *Deaf-Mutes' Journal* between the dates of September 1902 and February 1903 are referred to here by figures indicating the volume and number of issue.

A Beautiful Memorial Service at St. Matthew's Church, N.Y.C. DMJ 31/44.

All Angels' Mission for Deaf-Mutes, Trinity Parish, Chicago. DMJ 33/5.

All Souls' Church for the Deaf, Philadelphia. DMJ 31/43.

Brooklyn Guild, Brooklyn, N.Y. *In Memoriam.* DMJ 31/48.

Church Mission to Deaf-Mutes. *Memorial minutes* adopted at the Nov. 10, 1902 meeting. DMJ 32/46.

Death of Dr. T. Gallaudet. THE BRITISH DEAF MONTHLY, v. 11, no. 131—September 1902.

Draper, Amos. Thomas Gallaudet. AAD 47:393-403 (1903).

Editorial: *Rev. Thomas Gallaudet.* DMJ 31/35.

Fox, Thomas F. Obituary notes in the Proceedings of the 17th meeting of the Convention of American Instructors of the Deaf, Morganton, N.C. 1905.

Gallaudet, Virginia B. A Letter in reply to Fanwood. DMJ 31/42.

Gallaudet, Virginia B. A reply to a letter of sympathy from New England Gallaudet Association of Deaf-Mutes. DMJ 31/40.

Gilby, (Rev'd) D. Letter to the Rev. Austin W. Mann. DMJ 31/44.

Hagadorn, Junon. *The Best of Friends Has Gone to Rest* (poem). DMJ 31/37.

Hodgson, Edwin A. *Rev. Thomas Gallaudet, D.D., L.H.D.* AAD 55:39—1910.

Johnson, Dr. *Lessons From the Life of Dr. Gallaudet.* DMJ 31/38.

Jones, William G. *Life of Rev. Dr. Thomas Gallaudet.* DMJ 31/42.

Kenner, Marcus. *A Tribute.* DMJ 31/37.

Lindsley, Lucy Ornsky. *In Memoriam: Rev. Dr. Gallaudet.* DMJ 32/8.

Maine Deaf Mission. *In Memoriam.*. DMJ 31/45.

Mann, (Rev'd) A. W. Memorial Service, Chicago. DMJ 31/38.

Morehouse, Edgar P. *A Memorial to Rev. Gallaudet.* DMJ 31/42.

New England Gallaudet Association of Deaf-Mutes, 1902 convention at Bellow Falls, Vermont. *In Memoriam.* DMJ 31/38.

New England Industrial School for Deaf-Mutes, Beverly, Mass. *In Memoriam.* DMJ 32/4.

New York Historical Society, New York. *Letter to Mrs. Thomas Gallaudet.* Oct. 8, 1902. From private collection.

Perry, (Rev'd) Thomas D. *A Suitable Memorial.* DMJ 31/44.

St. Agnes' Mission at Grace Church, Cleveland, Ohio. *Memorial.* DMJ 32/10.

St. Andrew's Church/Mission, Boston & New England. Resolutions. DMJ 31/48.

St. Mark's Church for Deaf-Mutes, Brooklyn, N.Y. DMJ 31/41.

St. Mark's Mission, Cincinnati, Ohio. *A Memorial.* DMJ 31/49.

The Churchman. Necrology. Sept. 6, 1902.

The Gallaudet Club, meeting and Memorial Service. DMJ 31/39.

Wright Street Mission, Australia, *In Memoriam.* 31/50.

--By Henry L. Buzzard

INDEX